Life doesn't add up but opens up.

PRAISE FOR *THE BOOK OF SOUL*

"Mark Nepo has long been one of my favorite spiritual writers, and *The Book of Soul* is further proof why. It's filled with breathtaking lines you'll want to linger over, commit to memory, and carry with you. I recommend it for all of us wanting to stay connected to a deeper purpose as we rush through our days."

—Melinda Gates, *New York Times* bestselling
author of *The Moment of Lift*

"It's easy in these times to allow ourselves to slip into resignation, isolation, or despair. *The Book of Soul* is an antidote, a path that leads us back to our own wisdom and intuition and to the authentic truth of our souls."

—Arianna Huffington, founder & CEO of Thrive
Global and founder of *The Huffington Post*

"In *The Book of Soul*, Mark Nepo reminds us how rare it is to be here at all and how precious, real, and raw our tether to this life and each other. The insights gathered here will help you negotiate the currents of life while resting in the barest of simplicities. This book will strengthen your soul."

—Joan Borysenko, author of *The PlantPlus Diet
Solution* and *Your Soul's Compass*

"Mark Nepo has written another generous and valuable call to truth—at once inspiring, enlightening, empowering, and humbling. His words and the spaces between them remind me to slow down, to explore the still unfinished and awkward places in my life, and to honor and surrender to what is sacred, pure, and often confounding but always true about being human. Nepo's commitment to transform the tumble and grist of life into insights and understandings helps me improve my life."

—George Cappannelli, co-founder of AgeNation

ALSO BY MARK NEPO

THE BOOK OF SOUL

52 PATHS
TO LIVING WHAT MATTERS

MARK NEPO

ST. MARTIN'S
ESSENTIALS
NEW YORK

First published in the United States by St. Martin's Essentials,
an imprint of St. Martin's Publishing Group

www.stmartins.com

Designed by Steven Seighman

See page 265 for permissions.

The Library of Congress Cataloging-in-Publication Data is available upon request.

ISBN 978-1-250-26296-7 (paper over board)
ISBN 978-1-250-26302-5 (ebook)

Our books may be purchased in bulk for promotional, educational,
or business use. Please contact your local bookseller or the Macmillan
Corporate and Premium Sales Department at 1-800-221-7945, extension
5442, or by email at MacmillanSpecialMarkets@macmillan.com.

First Edition: May 2020

10 9 8 7 6 5

CONTENTS

OUR TRUE INHERITANCE

WIDENING OUR CIRCLE

HELPING EACH OTHER STAY AWAKE

Don't you want to be alive before you die?

—ANTHONY DOERR

Who will speak these days,
if not I,
if not you?

—MURIEL RUKEYSER

THE BOOK OF SOUL

Where All Souls Meet

After being born physically, we unfold within a second womb, meant to incubate our better angel. The second womb is an experiential one that, through the labor of a lifetime, births the soul on Earth. This book explores that process of transformation in its mystery, difficulty, and inevitability. Because things that matter are vast and timeless, I offer each chapter as a different path by which a soul can drink from what matters. And because things that matter take time, I've designed this journey as a weekly reader, to be entered a chapter each week over the course of a year, so you can weave your inner reflection into your days, letting one inform the other.

This dynamic transformation—how we are revealed and shaped by experience—connects two of my recent books. By living *The One Life We're Given*, we release the wisdom that waits in our heart, and that tender, human process leads us to *The Way Under the Way: The Place of True Meeting*. When we commit to these holy engagements that join who we are with the world, we discover that the temple is the world. This is the central inquiry of this book: how we inhabit the soul on Earth through a messy human life, living tenderly and authentically enough that we can be who we are everywhere and create a path to what matters.

Eventually, all the love, suffering, and humility we go through wear away our walls of resistance until Spirit shines from within us like an inner sun. This is how Spirit is revealed on Earth—as the coverings we carry are worn away by life, the light we carry can pour into the world.

Our constant challenge is to accept how life wears away what doesn't matter until the miracle of life is revealed in everything. Once living this barely in the open, our work is to let the light of Spirit come through, never thinking that we own it, but letting it use us to brighten and warm the hearts of others. This is the purpose of the human journey: to live openly and honestly until we become a source of uncovered light. Then life pours forth to renew us and all we meet.

Like a comet reduced to its center by the time it reaches Earth, the gravity of our journey leaves us bare and unadorned as we reach the simple, enduring center where all souls meet. To live so fully, we have to summon the courage to take off our armor and let things in. Then the soul has a chance to show itself. Through our immersion in being here and our devotion to do so kindly, we begin to enliven our compassion. This helps us endure our walk in the world.

The human tribe, at its best, is resilient, and, at its worst, relentlessly stubborn. We've spent centuries trying to keep things apart, when everything in life wants to come together. We've worked hard to separate light from dark, when together they form the threshold of depth. We've tried desperately to separate beauty from suffering, when it's beauty that softens our suffering. We've willfully insisted on separating good from bad, when the heart burns both in the fire of compassion. And in our terror, we're frantic to separate life from death, when each soul on Earth is a conduit between them. Every part of life is an intersection and emblem of all life. As a seed carries a fully grown tree and a spark ignites the life of fire, we each carry the shimmer of all there is.

We do need to separate things, not to alter life, but to move through life, the way a swimmer parts the deep. Though as soon as we finish a stroke, the Whole of Life joins around us. So the goal is not to control or conquer life, but to immerse ourselves in it. And for all the places we can travel and all the ways we can study, there's no greater teacher than when we dare to share the truth of our lives. When facing what's ours to face, we're surprised to learn, time and again, that under what seems unbearable is the rest of life waiting to be lived.

In time, the inexhaustible Universe can touch anyone brave enough and tender enough to embark on a quest to know who we are in relation to everything around us. Whether you call that vastness God, Atman, dharma, Allah, nature, or quantum physics, each of us can be infused with what matters if we can face the truth of our lives, love each other in spite of and because of our differences, and live into the deeper questions through acts of love.

Our journey from innocence to experience is how we emerge from the second womb. The fifty-two chapters of this book mark the passages we all face in moving through this experiential unfolding: enduring our walk in the world until we discover our true inheritance, which lets us live in the open by widening our circle until we help each other stay awake. The arc of this transformative journey is inescapable. We venture out only to discover the truth we carry within. And this exposure of depth and truth gives us the strength to open ourselves further in the world—until we use the ore we find inside to shape and repair the world.

Though no one can endure, discover, open, or stay awake for us, we are inextricably knit together. While you're discovering, I may be enduring. While I'm awake, you may be struggling to open. But your discovery helps me endure, as my wakefulness helps you open. We're linked in our humanity the way the earth holds a tree, so that tree can hold a nest, so that nest can hold a bird, so that bird can drop a seed that will in time give birth to the next tree. All our attempts seed each other.

To learn from life and its web of relationship, we are constantly challenged to stay in conversation with the moments of our lives. And so, I invite you to listen and reflect your way through this book, one chapter per week, and to write your way through the topics and stories by way of a journal. To help with this process, I offer "Questions to Walk With" at the end of each chapter. The doorway of questions here refers to a field of inquiry that includes but goes beyond literal questions. These sections include prompts to self-reflect in your journal as well as entry points to dialogue with a trusted friend or loved one.

It seems the purpose of suffering is to exhaust us of our differences, and the purpose of love is to awaken us to how we're at heart the same. Then we discover that the temple is the world. Still, every life, every generation, every age takes its turn at pushing each other away, only to be loved and worn back to the one tribe we belong to. This seems even more relevant in our tense, modern world. For there is no "they." We are they. We are each other. And there's a deep Unity that always waits below our righteous insistence that we know the way.

So, yes, we can talk, but ultimately we make no ground until we listen—to each other and to the current of humanity from which we rise and return. We only have one turn at being here together before we pass what we've done or not done to the next generation. I pray we can listen to what love and suffering open us to, so we can drink from that well and build a better world.

OUR WALK IN THE WORLD

The more you cut the branches of a tree, the higher and stronger it grows. The more you put the gold in the fire, the purer it becomes. The more you sharpen the steel by grinding, the better it cuts. . . . Therefore I am happy that you have had great tribulations and difficulties. . . . Strange it is that I love you and still I am happy that you have sorrows.

—Abdu'l-Bahá

We're shaped by what we go through, hollowed out by the storms of time. And the speed of the modern age only intensifies the pull of existence. Against these wearing forces, we have enduring tools to rely on, such as the ability to be wholehearted, the resilience through which we're informed by what we love, and the chance to be immersed in life and devoted to living. As we move repeatedly from surviving to thriving, our walk in the world can wear us down or lift us up, depending on how often we remember that we're part of something larger, depending on how thoroughly we can bathe trouble in the well of our soul. Yet no one can do any of this alone. It's letting each other in that can distribute the weight of suffering, which no one can escape. It's holding each other in our pain that can invoke the resting place of being that always surprises us. Our walk in the world is always precarious, as we find our way between burden and grace, falling down and getting up as many times as necessary.

The chapters in this section explore what it means to live with truth, meaning, and kindness, not abstractly but in a personal way. These are the antidotes for despair. When we can slow down enough, what we hide loses its reason to hide, and everything becomes holy. Then what's real moves between us, and what matters is everywhere. We still have to keep warm and pay the bills and face losing things we love. But our immersion and devotion and our return to presence make it all bearable, even beautiful at times.

1

LIVING WITH MEANING, TRUTH, AND KINDNESS

We are people hungry for life . . . [And] all you get
for this enormous effort is more life.

—ROBERT SEDER

THE MESSY MIRACLE we walk through called life is fragile and
resilient, ever-present and never guaranteed. Love moves us toward the miracle, while fear moves us toward the mess. And
since fear gets its power from not looking, we are called, no
matter our circumstance, to enlist the strength of heart to look
through our fears. Fear is a mood to be moved through, not a
voice to be obeyed. And there is always another direction on the
other side of pain and disappointment, if we can take a breath
and look around, the way a fish, given the chance, will always
swim toward light.

Meaning, truth, and kindness are our constant teachers.
They help us live through fear, pain, and disappointment.
They are flames that light the heart. Still, we all know that

flames burn as well as give off light. In just this way, every inner teacher has a burning quality that we must endure in order to receive their light. We can consider these experiences the growth pains of transformation.

By its very nature, meaning is gathered and enlivened through relationship. It is how we make sense of our experiences, the practice of living as an awakened part in an awakened Whole.

By its nature, truth is gathered and enlivened through deep presence and deep listening. It is the practice of seeing and receiving things-as-they-are, the practice of living with the bareness of being.

And kindness is enlivened and released through the risk of immediate care. It is the practice of allowing compassion to guide us, the practice of uncovering our intimacy with all things.

Together, meaning, truth, and kindness connect everything, forming a lifeline we can hold on to, no matter the storm.

The long conversation of this book is offered as a way to personalize your own relationship with meaning, truth, and kindness—as a way to personalize your very specific practice of living as an awakened part in an awakened Whole, as a way to personalize your individual practice of living with the bareness of being, and as a way to personalize your own evolving practice of being intimate with all things.

Meaning, truth, and kindness are our
constant teachers. . . . They are flames
that light the heart.

Questions to Walk With

- In your journal, describe your ongoing conversation between possibility and disappointment. Which has your ear now? How would you describe the larger rhythms of life that include both possibility and disappointment?

- In conversation with a friend or loved one, describe a recent appearance in your life of meaning, truth, or kindness and how this has affected you.

2

THE SPEED OF OUR AGE

WHEN WE BECOME entranced with what is inconsequential, we stop listening to what matters. This is how worry feeds itself, how it fills us with psychic noise.

It's especially difficult to hear what matters in our modern age. Given our preoccupation with efficiency and productivity, it takes a quiet courage to silence our worry and agitation when we're always being told that we're falling short. Being constantly minimized makes us insecure until we swarm like lost and hungry bees for any hive that might soothe our pain of being less—less than perfect, less than beautiful, less than enough, less than what everyone expects of us, inevitably less than our dreams of love and peace.

To counter the speed of our age, we're asked to open our heart wherever we are. Even though, in the press of the modern world, such softness and openness can be mistaken for being lazy, aimless, and without purpose. But sometimes we need to drift and be aimless in order to disengage the frenzy of civilization and put down our worried agendas, so we can re-connect to the underlying reality that informs everything.

Harder still, we live in an age so obsessed with the new that we've been called the "disposable society." Though it's often easier to throw something out than repair it, we lose our relationship to the things around us if we discard them without honoring them. When we dispose of things without a thought, we lose the history of objects and tools and the presence they accumulate for moving through our lives. When we miss the story of touch that ordinary things carry, we lose access to the continuity of being that joins us all. The antidote to speed is to hold things and ask for their stories.

In time, not listening to what matters lets us become pre-occupied with the noise of the world until the noise of our minds becomes an ingrained pattern. It helps here to under-stand how the brain creates patterns of what we know and how we move—from the want to quench a physical thirst, to how the arm then lifts and reaches for a cup of water, to the want to be loved and how the heart then opens and reaches for all that is lovable.

Neurons are bits of information stored in the brain. The energy patterns that connect the bits of information are synapses. The neurons and the synapses that connect them form neural networks, which the brain returns to and uses again. Once established, the synapses that connect neurons begin to solidify into the patterned response they form together. This makes fast work of reaching for something to drink the second time, or lifting the groceries when the checkout person hands them to us, or recognizing the *beep* in the morning as the alarm that our groggy arm needs to turn off. In this way, the brain relies on its neural networks to create and access daily functions stored in our memory, so we don't have to relearn every little thing, again and again, each time we encounter it.

But the further we get from physical neural networks, the less this works. As we move into psychological and social neural networks, we cease to take in new information and our response to a new situation is often based on old patterns of information—old measurements, if you will. So when a stranger who has exactly what I need to learn has the tone of voice of my mother who wounded me, I might shut her down and walk away. Relied on too heavily, these mental and emotional neural networks, if unchecked, become ruts in the brain. They then form the basis for preconceptions, at the least, and prejudice, at the worst—till we mistake our patterned responses for unshakable truth. As William James said, "A great many people think they are thinking when they are merely rearranging their prejudices." And as the sculptor Karen French confides, "I'm haunted that my beliefs are just the thoughts I keep thinking."

We are all prey to this. No one can sidestep it. The stubborn reflexes of our deeply personal neural networks are not about everyone else, but directly about us. How we break these patterns and create new ones has everything to do with what we listen to—whether we experience life directly or simply react to shadows in our own hall of experiential mirrors.

So while considering the speed and noise of our efficient and disposable world, while considering how our brains make habits of our reactions, let's look at three more ways of not listening: judgment, illusion, and the appetite for more.

Judging others overlays the truth of what is with a screen of our preferred conclusions. For judgment, the kind that debases and elevates, distances us from the experience of others. It keeps us from learning the truth of what's before us. For example, when I judge a friend who is late as not caring, I may never know that they stopped to help a stranger who fell along the way. In time, the cost of such judgment is that it becomes a clear wall we construct around ourselves to make others think there is no wall, until they go to touch us or we reach out and no one can get through. To see and not be touched drains us of our aliveness—like smelling fruit without ever being able to eat it.

I remember a professor in graduate school who judged all modern poetry as outside the rigor and excellence of the classics. He denigrated all contemporary attempts at expression. When his wife died suddenly, I offered him an anthology of poems about loss and grief filled with some of the most gifted and compassionate voices of our age. Though I could see the face under his face tremble, he coldly thanked me and tossed the book in the garbage. More than being rude, he was sealing himself within his clear wall of judgment, ensuring his deep loneliness in a place no one could reach.

Illusion stems from forcing our preferred understanding of life on all the situations we meet, as we become more interested in sameness than growing. Working to sustain illusion is its own hell. I remember watching a polo match years ago when a horse broke its leg. The far side of the field was where the club members sat. Two field boys with puffy sleeves ran out to hold up a blanket, shielding the club members from the fallen horse, as we on the other side of the field watched someone shoot the horse in the head. Holding up the blanket to shield the club members is a metaphor for the effort to sustain illusion, to pretend that life is other than it is, while in reality the blanket is not shielding anything.

And the appetite for more is as old as time. In ancient Greece, *pleonektein*, from which we get the word "pleonexia," referred to a condition in which a person lived with an insatiable appetite for more of everything. The Christian theologian William Barclay defined pleonexia as a cursed love of having. Plato and Aristotle thought this condition to be the source of greed. This is a dangerous form of not listening that plagues the modern world. It speaks to our "fill-'er-up" society in which we think eating will keep us from the threshold of emptiness, and noise will keep us from the threshold of silence, and adventure will keep us from the threshold of being ordinary. When all the while, it's through the thresholds of emptiness, silence, and being ordinary that the true gifts of being alive wait to be discovered.

None of this is easy. And with so many ways of not listening, we can easily miss our next teacher. Still, the true gifts of being alive show themselves in the simplest things that wait at every corner underneath the speed of our age. Our next teacher could be in a breeze that crosses our face, asking us to turn. And when we turn, we might be seized by the light in a certain way. And through that light, we might see the face of someone we're supposed to love. But if we don't turn, we won't meet the person we're supposed to love. It doesn't mean we will never know love. We just might wind up missing what we're supposed to learn.

All the spiritual traditions ask us to listen, that is, to move closer to what matters through the work of being, and to quiet the noise in our mind so we can return to an unscripted moment where the glow and pulse of life can show itself. All the contemplative practices ready us for the space that is stung open when a father dies or a dream shatters or we find ourselves in exile or put upon—and there's nothing to do except sit and be with the mystery of what is. The only way to silence the speed and noise of the tiger is to sit before the world with an open heart as our lives finally open.

The antidote to speed is to hold things and ask for their stories.

QUESTIONS TO WALK WITH

- In your journal, describe the most judgmental person you know and how this creates a wall around them. Then describe one way you are judgmental and how it keeps you from experiencing life.

- In conversation with a friend or loved one, describe one way the speed of our age affects you, and one step you can take to be more in your own life.

3

ALWAYS PART OF SOMETHING LARGER

Life is the greatest storyteller.
—MN

NO MATTER WHAT we're going through, faith in life means believing that there's always more beyond the condition of our understanding—the way the rest of the Universe whirls beyond the light of any given star. In just this way, we're always part of something larger than our condition, and the circumstance we're in—real and consuming as it can be—is not the condition of the Whole.

Faith in this distinction allows for healing. Because, as enough water will dilute poison, enough of life will dilute pain and fear and worry. While it's up to us to see it through, unmitigated life will in time mitigate the edge and press of what is difficult. This is why it's crucial to open when we're closed, so life can do what's inherent to its nature: restore itself. Inevitably, what we face is always real *and* there's always an edge where what we face drops off into the vastness of life that is just continuing.

When I feel small, life won't make me large, but letting life in will dissipate my smallness. Then it's my work to re-find my worth. This is how we partner with life: it gives and we receive. Then we inhabit our worth and give back, the way plants and humans exchange oxygen and carbon dioxide. In this way, the vastness, indifferent as it is, remains life-giving.

None of this will prevent us from suffering or from the cascade of circumstance we face for being human. Yet this journey appears differently for every person. And it's the very personal initiation of experience and erosion of our stubbornness that lets our true nature show itself. Until, accepting our true nature, we gain access to our gifts.

We all struggle between the narrow condition of our understanding and the vastness continuing around us. As soon as we succumb to our narrow condition, whatever it might be, as soon as we stop receiving life, we begin to paint everything with the color of our trouble. This is how we can listen to another without truly hearing them, how we can touch something beautiful and overlay it with where we've been or where we think we're going, and miss its beauty.

Under the press of our particular condition, we can end up drifting into the past or the future, while stepping about as a ghost in the moment at hand. You can tell when someone is not where they are. Their sentences never quite finish. They seem to look through everyone they meet. Their eyes are like balloons let go of. We've all done this. So the challenge isn't to criticize but to course-correct.

When I find myself drifting into the future or dwelling in the past, I close my eyes and start over, trying to bring all of me to whatever is there when I open them again. I vow to look at one thing at a time, like a child. I vow to listen more closely, like a person gone blind. I vow to rediscover the world in whatever gritty, precious thing is before me. And to quiet my mind, so I might feel the vastness of life flowing between us.

It helps to tell stories. I share this one because Tom's story is our story. Tom is an architect who feels very lost. Today he's leaving work, entering the elevator on the fiftieth floor, alone in the metal box taking him back to the ground, stopping along the way to gather others. As he descends, he leans against the wall of the elevator, wondering how he came to be so tired and lost. Tom is a man who started out in innocence, but as he tried to love, he was hurt. As he tried to help others, he was manipulated and betrayed. Tom began with a sublime trust in life but became jaded and fearful. What he doesn't know is that when he's afraid, he forgets what he knows. When he fears situations, he forgets what he's learned about moving through the world. When he fears he's lost his way, he forgets who he is. When he fears the world is lacking, he forgets the gift of life.

Floor by floor, Tom descends. He wonders if tomorrow will be any different. What he doesn't know is that when he fears there won't be enough, he becomes greedy. When he fears those around him, he becomes cruel. When he fears he's not enough, he inflates himself, becoming larger than he is, and starts knocking things over and wanting things that aren't his.

The elevator opens on the ground floor, and Tom walks into the street where the late sun curls around the buildings to spill upon his face. He stops and closes his eyes. It's the best he's felt all day. Standing there in the late light, Tom begins to quiet his fear and starts to remember how to move through the world. Walking a few blocks in the light, he starts to remember who he is. As he begins to listen to the sky, he starts to remember the gift of life.

Each of us struggles between being insular and making our way in the world. One more story that is our story: On a dreary day, a vital, thoughtful woman starts to build a tall, thick wall. She thinks she's building a castle, but in time it becomes a prison. Though she thinks the wall keeps everything out, surprise in time curls over the top like a cloud and circles her head like a fog. And sorrow in time seeps through the cracks of her wall like a distant memory that lodges in her ear. And forgetting that she built the castle-turned-prison, she puts her sad ear to the wall and listens for life on the other side.

Those who love her haven't given up. They pound on the wall for her to come out, but she can hardly hear them. No one knows what pain or argument sent her into exile within herself. But after a while, life leaves her alone. Until on a breezy day, the song of two birds circling each other drifts through the keyhole of her castle-turned-prison and some part of her has to see those birds. As she opens the weighty door of her own making, the vastness returns and life kisses her forehead as she weeps at how much beauty she has missed.

Unmitigated life will in time mitigate the edge and press of what is difficult. This is why it's crucial to open when we're closed.

Questions to Walk With

- In your journal, describe a current difficulty and then describe the vastness of life continuing around you in your difficulty. How does life outside of your experience affect you and what you're going through?

- In conversation with a friend or loved one, describe a time when you inflated yourself. Why wasn't being who you are enough in that situation? What was the result of being other than who you are?

4

IMMERSION AND DEVOTION

I BELIEVE IN the spiritual qualities of immersion and devotion. They've guided and saved my life more than once. From the time I was little, I would stare at bits of life happening and get lost in life unfolding. I remember watching a fly against our bathroom window for the longest time trying to get out into the light. And watching the hawk nesting in the large oak behind our house until it seemed to stare back at me. Or sitting with my father in silence as we watched the winter waves froth and curl against the docks in Lindenhurst, New York. My father had the biggest smile when beckoned by the sea. These were early tastes of immersion and devotion. Since then, I've realized that it takes effort to stay immersed until wonder reveals itself, and devotion to stay immersed until wonder becomes a way of life.

The word "immerse" comes from the Latin, meaning "to dip in." The word "devote" comes from the Latin, meaning "to uphold a vow." So while immersion invokes the giving of ourselves completely to an endeavor until it reveals its meaning, devotion asks that we uphold our commitment to stay immersed in that which has meaning.

Immersion and devotion are at the heart of my life as a teacher. I began teaching in a rural high school in upstate New York. After four years, I went to graduate school, where, on a fellowship, I taught classes. After receiving my doctorate, I taught at the State University of New York at Albany for eighteen years. In all those years of teaching I wouldn't have given grades if I didn't have to. At the beginning of every semester, I told my students that the realms we would be entering were eternal and dynamic and full of great rewards that would serve them for a lifetime. I told them that journeying there would be more valuable than any grade they could achieve. Of course, no one believed me. I would say that anyone could get an A if they immersed themselves completely. I had no problem giving the entire class A's. I told them my dream was to have an entire class immersed. I also said that the only way to fail was to withhold their full attention, to withhold their devotion.

In twenty-four years of teaching, I found repeatedly, with few exceptions, that as soon as students gave their full attention, they became immersed. As soon as they became immersed, they put in more effort and time than if they were studiously working for a grade. Time and again, I found that students, once immersed for their own reasons, did much more than I asked of them. All of this is evidence that learning is an act of devotion in itself, which is more rewarding and useful than any particular piece of information learned.

As we give our full attention to anything over a lifetime, the fantasy of reward and the grandiosity of creating something great or lasting evaporate, though we might create something useful and durable beyond our own personhood. When we can see our effort through, beyond the goal that gets us started, immersion and devotion become the practice that lets us experience Eternity. The end of that practice is our own transformation: we become one with what we work toward.

I imagine the naturalist John James Audubon's eyes began to widen and open like a bird after all those years of sketching feathers. I imagine the impressionist Claude Monet began to paint the floaters in his eyes after all those years of following light. I imagine the marine biologist Rachel Carson began to lose herself in the rain after staring at the sea until it told the story of its beginning. I imagine the New York City photographer Garry Winogrand began taking pictures with his heart, which may be why he left sixty-six hundred rolls of undeveloped film when he died. I imagine Michelangelo began to feel the statue in his heart come alive after a lifetime of releasing the veins he saw in marble. I imagine Carl Jung began to speak unknowingly from the well of all souls after rowing his way into the sea of the Unconscious. And I imagine Albert Einstein felt armless and weightless after peeling back his life to the weightless vantage point of relativity.

If we let ourselves experience immersion, whatever we love over time becomes a garden. And if devoted to that garden, what we turn over year after year becomes our teacher. The mystery of deep living is that we become life itself.

Learning is an act of devotion in itself,
which is more rewarding and useful than
any particular piece of information learned.

QUESTIONS TO WALK WITH

- In conversation with a friend or loved one, describe someone you admire for their devotion. Discuss the nature of their devotion and how it seems to affect the life of their heart and the lives of those around them.

5

THE PULL OF EXISTENCE

WE LIVE IN a technological age overrun with fragmentation and isolation, because our preoccupation with everything mechanical has divorced us from the Whole of Life. There is nothing wrong with technology or the digital gifts of our age. But technology is inert. And just as water fills a hole because of gravity, existence will rush to fill us and overwhelm us if we don't meet the outer world with an inner life. So, if not committed to inhabiting our inwardness and developing a set of inner values, the characteristics of technology—moving too fast, being in more than one place at a time, never standing still, multitasking, and being insular—will become our inner values by default.

Sidetracked by values we assume rather than choose, dreams never get built and ruins never get rebuilt, as our lives meander from their initiations of transformation. Exiled by our inexorable will imposing itself everywhere, the Mystery itself must hover in the sky like a lonely god cut loose from a culture that no longer believes in mystery. To such an ancient force, we must seem like erratic ants that never stand still. And what we do to each other when lost is carving a face in the Earth that those more caring than we will have to read.

For centuries, since the pernicious building of the Tower of Babel, we've been miseducated toward valuing things over people. And our obsession with living a successful life over an embodied life blocks us from the strength love can give us. The Hindu philosopher and teacher Jiddu Krishnamurti (1895–1986) said:

> *Our present education is rotten because it teaches us to love success and not what we are doing. The result has become more important than the action. You know, it is good . . . to be kind without a name. . . . You are just a creative human being living anonymously, and in that there is richness and great beauty.*

We might better learn from fish, who travel in schools quite naturally. For the true aim of schooling is to move through the deep, along with others, by taking what is essential through our gills. When we're authentic to our own nature, to our own questions, to our own experience, we travel together quite naturally. It's our authenticity that keeps us together, side by side. While our refusal to be authentic, out of fear or pain, is what alienates us until we feel that life is random and that we are alone.

Eventually, we're called to meet outer with inner, to love what we do more than what we achieve, and to travel with those who are authentic, even when we're clumsy and awkward. So never let what you believe in be snuffed because people around you don't seem to understand. There are many ways to remedy the chaotic forces in our world.

Every time you're kind to a stranger and help another up, every time you speak your truth and listen to another, you are keeping the fire of humanity lit. This is the lineage that has kept the world going through times of great disturbance. Being true to what you care about and standing up for those less fortunate will always make a difference.

Existence will rush to fill us and overwhelm us if we don't meet the outer world with an inner life.

Questions to Walk With

- In your journal, describe the difference, as you experience it, between loving success and loving what you do.

- In conversation with a friend or loved one, tell the story of a time when caring for another helped bring your inwardness out to meet the world.

6

Being Wholehearted

Why not call the moment of certainty, the fleeting
moment when everything that ever lived is right behind
my pounding heart, why not call that moment: Beat-of-
the-thousand-wings-of-God-inside-my-chest. . . .

—MN

Just as a bird can't glide on the wind unless it's wings are
spread, being wholehearted is the only way to be lifted by the
mystical web of life. This ever-present sweep of life-force is an
endless resource that requires all of who we are to access. We
don't have to explore this very far to realize that being wholehearted or half-hearted affects both the individual soul and the
life of our community. And so the work of being human is to be
all-embracing, to bring our entire self to whatever we're given.

The more we withhold, the more random life appears. This
is not a matter of reward or punishment, but cause and effect,
as when a bird tucks its wings and starts to fall from the sky.
Likewise, we need to keep looking until the water goes still, or

the lake will not reflect the sky above our head. And pulling back from life too soon will have us wake in what appears to be a disconnected world.

The work of remaining wholehearted depends on the honest acceptance of all our gifts and failings. Difficult as this may be, we can only access our compassion by being whole, which means not denying the difficult or stubborn parts of who we are. When spacious enough to be a home for our full humanity, two treasures open up. First, we're allowed to experience the full miracle of life, and second, we're allowed to experience the full miracle of love.

This commitment to Wholeness works on the societal level as well. A wholehearted community is one that doesn't deny its flaws or shortcomings but works toward an honest acceptance of both its strengths and failed attempts in living up to its values. When a community is spacious enough to be a home for all its citizens, the frail and stubborn alike, a healthy society emerges.

We can't go very far here without acknowledging Carl Jung. It was Jung who pioneered our current understanding of how we avoid and deny aspects of ourselves. He spoke of our un-wanted psychic material as our shadow. Our shadow is not necessarily good or bad. It simply mirrors and exaggerates the refused dimensions of our personality. Jung emphasized the importance of incorporating our shadow into our conscious awareness. Otherwise we project these exaggerated attributes onto others.

Jung discovered that the more we deny any one aspect of who we are, the more powerful and distorted its place in our life. For example, the more we deny our need to take genuine risks, the more we might develop an addiction to gambling. In general, the more we deny our humanity, the less aware we are of the abundance of life and the generosity of others.

The projection of unwanted psychic material plagues most communities, as well. In modern America, we push away what we most fear in ourselves. For instance, in the last fifteen years, many of the members of Congress who were most vocal against gay rights were exposed as being secretly gay. Consider as well the way we make pariahs out of the homeless and the sick, because of our fear of being homeless and sick. And how our fear of emotion and intimacy escalates a subculture of pornography and affairs.

The extreme violence that permeates our culture rises, in great degree, from our insistence as a society on repressing our life of feeling. Since the need to open and feel is innate and can't be denied, it shows up sideways in movies of people being literally blown open. The more we push these vulnerable and unwanted aspects of ourselves away, the stronger their distorted appearance becomes.

A wholehearted person tries to honor and join the seemingly separate parts that live within them. A wholehearted society tries to honor and join the seemingly separate citizens that live within it. Wholehearted integrity is inclusive, a matter of welcome and congruence. This is not an abstract issue. Being wholehearted or half-hearted has real consequences. In Trosly-Breuil, France, L'Arche is a lay community where people with developmental disabilities and those who care for them live together. Jean Vanier, the celebrated founder of L'Arche, spoke to what he learned about true relationship from living there:

> As long as we refuse to accept that we are a mixture of light
> and darkness, of positive qualities and failings, of love and

hate, of altruism and egocentricity, of maturity and im-
maturity, and that we are all children of the same Father
[I would say Unity of Life —MN], we will continue to
divide the world into enemies (the "baddies") and friends
(the "goodies"). We will go on throwing up barriers around
ourselves and our communities, spreading prejudice.

As long as we separate ourselves into "baddies" and "goodies," we avoid the terrible and inevitable fact that we are capable of all we encounter. Creating "baddies" is a form of cultural shadow by which we banish those who remind us of aspects we don't want to look at in ourselves. The venerable Vietnamese monk Thich Nhat Hanh held up the truth of this in his poem "Please Call Me by My True Names." This poem was provoked when one of the Vietnamese boat people, a twelve-year-old girl, drowned herself in the ocean after being raped by a sea pirate. Here is an excerpt:

I am the twelve-year-old girl,
refugee on a small boat,
who throws herself into the ocean
after being raped by a sea pirate.
And I am the pirate,
my heart not yet capable
of seeing and loving. . . .

Please call me by my true names,
so I can hear all my cries and laughter at once,
so I can see that my joy and pain are one.

Please call me by my true names,
so I can wake up

and the door of my heart
could be left open,
the door of compassion.

We must not confuse what is being said here. Understanding the worst in each other—and how that capacity lives in us as well—does not *dissipate* the need for justice. It *opens us* to the wisdom *waiting* in justice. In facing that we are each capable of great tenderness and great brutality, we open the door of our compassion and so *deepen* our capacity for justice. Perhaps the most enduring retribution for any of us is to mend the very thing we have brutalized. Perhaps the greatest justice is for the inhuman in us to become human again, until we can see what we have done with the softer eyes we were born with.

I think this is the unmapped ground of social healing that South Africa has awakened the world to with its brave work of truth and reconciliation. Longfellow said, "If we could read the secret history of our enemies we should find in each [person's] life sorrow and suffering enough to disarm all hostility." I wonder what he faced in himself that allowed him the grace of this perception. For we can only see as far into the world as we can see into ourselves. It stirs me to look into my own life, so I might polish my heart into a clear window through which to truly behold others.

This is all hard, crucial, and ancient work. In the Hindu myth, The Churning of the Ocean, the gods decide that they need the help of all the demons in order to churn and stir the "Ocean of Being" in order to bring forth the treasures of kindness and consciousness. It's instructive here that when forces and beings turn self-destructive and demonic, the gods do not slay them or imprison or exile them. They *enlist* them in a communal effort to stir the Ocean of Being until what surfaces is a shared, wholehearted consciousness. Together, the gods and demons become one restorative force known as Shakti or Durga.

As individuals and in community, this is the goal of wholeheartedness: to admit our failings, limitations, and darker impulses and to enfold them into a complete effort to restore kindness and Unity. This is a timeless task about which we have much to learn. But we can begin by accepting that we can't ignore, censure, or exile parts of our humanity or our community without suffering for pushing parts of ourselves into the darkness. We can begin by accepting our full humanity, while holding each other accountable for what we do, and helping each other repair the torn seams of the world.

We can only see as far into the world
as we can see into ourselves.

Questions to Walk With

- In conversation with a friend or loved one, describe someone you push away and explore why. Try to be honest about what unwanted part of yourself this person mirrors.

7

PUSHING ON

You don't need to be without fear to be brave.
—TAMI SIMON

I HEARD THIS story from a Peace Corps worker, just home from living for two years in Nigeria. The story comes from his closest friend there, Koofah. This happened while Koofah was traveling with a driver from the village of Akbuyo to Lagos, a city near the sea.

One night, when neither could sleep, Koofah told him, "It was widely known that one shouldn't travel at night through these regions. Cars have been known to be bombed and held up. Bandits will slit your throat. It was a six-hour drive and we'd planned enough time to make it to the sea by dusk. Along the way, near Fiditi, there was an accident. A truck hit the side of a car in front of me. The trucker was fine and went on his way without even getting out, but the man in the car was hurt. He had broken his shoulder and was cut up. We were afraid to move him. We made him comfortable and drove to the next town for help—an hour drive. We found the hospital and asked for an ambulance to be sent. But they didn't have an ambulance and there were no doctors in the hospital. They wouldn't be back for three days. Now I was stuck. I didn't know what to do. If we went back for him, we'd never cross the desert before nightfall. I told myself, it wasn't a completely barren road. Someone else would come along, and they would bring him to the hospital. Even so, there were no doctors. I didn't know what to do. I was afraid of falling prey in the night desert. I'm ashamed to say, I left him there. We kept our pace. I never knew what happened to him. It's been years, but to this day, I regret not going back."

Like so many of us, Koofah never found his courage. He resisted the impulse of kindness in his heart and is now caught replaying his missed opportunity forever.

Whether or not we stop to care for those we meet along the way frames the tipping point of our will. So often, we stand by our plans or our fears instead of standing by our core. So often, we hide in our neutrality, as if watching were a safe harbor somehow set outside of the storm and crash of life. Neutrality is really an illusion, more like my dog, who, when she hears thunder, tucks her nose in a corner, thinking she's invisible. It's how journalists long for the action of being embedded within armies waging war, as if their press passes will keep them from live fire. How often do we court danger, thinking we're embedded safely in our watching, thinking no one can reach us?

Often, we stand by our plans or our fears
instead of standing by our core.

QUESTIONS TO WALK WITH

- In conversation with a friend or loved one, describe a time when you pushed on instead of helping someone along the way. What made you push on? Now describe a time when someone pushed on from you. Finally, what would it take for you to stop and change your plans?

8

As Many Times As Necessary

SOMEWHERE ALONG THE way, we became obsessed with the new, preoccupied with breaking ground and never repeating ourselves. Yet the ocean reveals its power and mystery by repeating its waves around the world. Nature replenishes the Earth by repeating the cycle of the seasons. And we suffer and fall in love, learn and forget, and go numb and reawaken in the repetition of our human seasons. Ironically, the lessons of life come from inhabiting the authentic cycles of experience.

We all struggle with this tension between our obsession with making things new and the wisdom that comes from reentering life as many times as necessary in order for it to reveal its secrets.

How many times do we run from those we love because we insist on finding something new, when we're often being asked to live more deeply where we are? The same can be said for our work in the world. How often do we abandon what has meaning because we think we're bored, when we're actually being asked to penetrate the habit of work in order to unearth the very center of our calling.

I think this is what T. S. Eliot refers to when he says in his book of poems *Four Quartets*:

> *We shall not cease from exploration*
> *And the end of all our exploring*
> *Will be to arrive where we started*
> *And know the place for the first time.*

While there are clearly times we have to break free and enter the unknown, there are just as many times when it is imperative to lean more deeply into the heart of where we are and love what's in the way until the glow of life, uncovered, reanimates our way.

But being human, we hide and come forth, again and again. When we hide, nothing seems possible. When we come forth, everything seems possible. Like a whale that swims below and breaches above, we move from our solitude into the world and back. Still, no matter how often we lose our way, we have what we need. We are what we need. We have only to dive.

Mysteriously, it is our nakedness of being and heart that is the greatest form of sonar, leading us into a depth that always renews. And, I confess, when moving through time, I wonder how much is left. But entering time, there is abundance everywhere. Beautifully, this call and response between life and death is like two hands cupping the sun.

When we hide, nothing seems possible.
When we come forth, everything
seems possible.

QUESTIONS TO WALK WITH

- In conversation with a friend or loved one, describe a situation you have been asked to reenter or repeat, as many times as necessary, in order to learn and grow. Did you resist this journey or welcome it? What lesson finally revealed itself?

9

THE PRISON TREE

I TELL THESE stories as a Jew. Today, in Warsaw, Poland, near the ghetto where a thousand Jews with makeshift weapons held off the Nazis for twenty-eight days in the spring of 1943, there is only one wall remaining as it was. It is the east wall of the Mokotów Prison in Warsaw. Even more touching than preserving that wall is the old twisted tree in front of it. If you go there, no matter the season, you will find the tree tacked and nailed with letters and cards, each telling the story of a loved one, or the loved one of a loved one, who died in that prison or in the Warsaw Ghetto or while escaping.

If we look in our hearts, we'll find a prison tree in front of every wall. Our prisons are different, but the tree that grows outside it is always the same. Since the beginning of time, each prison tree preserves the stories that bind us and free us. I'm drawn to where all these stories touch.

In 2009, I went to Prague and wandered in the Old Jewish Cemetery. First used in 1439, more than twelve thousand gravestones are crammed into this courtyard where a hundred thousand people have been buried. The earth there swells and rolls like a sea churned in a storm, stones leaning every which way, scraping each other from behind, above, below, broken, worn of their names, one on top of the other for five hundred years, crumbled, buried twelve deep. This is the swell and crash of the Jewish soul in its fall through Eternity, anything but at rest, each pushing its stone into another: this one streaked with rain, another stained with earth, moss growing out of some, burn marks on others. Like muscles cut open in mid-lift, these labored souls show us how to lift.

I spent so many years pushing off my own tradition to shape my own mind, only to find that I belong in this ancient cemetery: churned, leaning, broken, strong. Everyone knows these souls are here and not here. From above, the storm has worn them down. From below, these spirits keep pushing the stones back into life. I walked by an old rabbi who smelled like my grandfather. I listened and listened, but no one speaks within those walls.

The next day I made my way to the Jewish Museum, where the deputy director, Michal Frankl, talked about the fate of Czech Jews. He told us in his delicate English that the camp at Terezín (1941–1945) was a demeaning purgatory, a waiting station for extermination camps such as Auschwitz.

He told us that a central burden of the Jewish Museum in Prague, created in 1906, is the troublesome fact that thousands of its precious objects come from Nazi cruelty and destruction. For the Czech Jewish culture was preserved because Hitler perversely intended for Prague to house a museum of an extinct people. So the question hovers in a dark cloud: How is it that good can come from cruelty? How are we to hold sacred objects spared by blunt and evil hands?

Director Frankl then introduced Helga Hošková-Weissová, a ninety-year-old artist who survived Terezín as a child. Helga began by saying that she doesn't like the word "survivor." Helga is a wise but simple woman, grounded in this life, an artist who would have rather painted other things. She told us that as a child in Terezín, her father gently told her to "draw what you see." Now, almost seventy years later, her son tells her, "Draw as long as you can see."

Helga wasn't sentimental, but her eyes were tender when talking of her childhood friend Anna, who whispered to her back then in a barracks that housed fifty, "Forget the hours of suffering, but not what they have taught you." How does a child become so wise unless robbed of her childhood? Helga told us how the Nazis tried to break their spirits with psychological taunts. They used hearses to carry wood and groceries, while wooden carts carried bodies. Life was turned upside down. She and the other children were forced to carry bread in a coffin.

When she returned after the war, one neighbor said matter-of-factly, "We didn't think you'd be coming back. We were short of food and sold your clock for soup. We're sorry." Another refused to say hello. Another refused to return property he took and was angry that she had returned. Her life as she'd known it had vanished.

In the years that followed, it was difficult to continue. Helga grew depressed and stopped painting for years because she didn't want to paint the Holocaust any longer and couldn't paint anything else. After a dark time, she finally accepted that Terezín was her theme and looked for "new life in the wreckage."

Even today, Helga's daughter asks, "Why is there not one picture I can hang in my home? Why are you so pessimistic?" Helga said, "I'm just painting what is there." This lesson is for all of us: Work with what you're given. Draw what you see. Find light in what is there.

A Rwandan in the audience asked Helga, "How could you return to your life when so many need to leave to go on?" Then, a Palestinian blurted out, "Have you been able to let the past rest?" And an African American asked, "How do I speak of slavery to my children without changing their view of life?"

Helga didn't understand the questions in English and turned to Director Frankl. They talked quietly in Czech. Then he translated, "She says, 'There's no one message from the Holocaust. The discussion itself that brings us to a more human way *is* the message.'"

Helga's drawings were published forty years after her confinement in Terezín at the request of German teachers who have become her friends. Now she speaks to German students. One asked her, "Should I be ashamed of being German?" She told him, "You're not to blame for the past. You're responsible for the future."

So much was stirred in me that I don't know where to begin. Something painful surfaced in me as I listened to Helga, as I watched the other faces in the room. I couldn't tell who was Jewish, but felt that I was not alone. And being in Europe, in Prague, so close to one of the centers of Jewish life and suffering, I realized how invisible I am as a Jew in America. I confess for the first time that I feel a particular burden in being so invisible. I can't know the pain of being African American or Islamic or Hispanic in America, and not being able to hide your heritage. But as a Jew, it's shameful to choose every day whether I will be known as a Jew or not.

It's a terrible post-Holocaust condition that we've been imprinted to believe that it's dangerous to be seen or heard. No one consciously taught me this. Still, the burden of being visible or not resurfaces day by day.

A profound paradox of the Holocaust continues to be that, for the most part, only those who were invisible survived. And all the while, being visible and resilient is such an integral part of the Jewish character. How to make sense of all this?

In a very deep and real way, each event in life is an occasion for us to explore and pronounce who we are, what we are, and where we come from. Each circumstance we meet replays these great conditions, which ripple like the life-and-death choice so many faced in World War II, still lapping from the psychic tsunami of the Holocaust—even two generations later and a continent away.

In a felt and troubling way, I'm beginning to see that the Holocaust is not an event we must relate to in the past, but some terrible earthquake in human decency whose impact is still sending its tremors under our feet. The truth is that without ever speaking about it, children born after the storm are always preparing for the storm.

Now I understand why I've never felt connected to any one place, why I've always carried a sense of exile, feeling no outer home. Now I understand that this sense of exile is tethered to and in some way generated by the unfathomable loss of the Holocaust.

Yet I felt a sense of home in that ancient cemetery in Prague. As I touched those broken graves, I dropped my guard and the endless preparedness that all Jews have. I am a Jew. Cultural? Religious? Practicing? Not? These descriptions are woefully inadequate. I only know that I love my grandfather's worn and frayed Talmud that he brought to America from Russia. That I love the endless river of question that the Mishnah points to. That staring into Roman Vishniac's photos, I see eyes long gone that I belong to. That in Abraham Heschel's voice I sense and taste the Mystery. I am a Jew, that's for certain. But what this means keeps unfolding like a sea that sends part of itself to shore while keeping its depth away from all shores.

I can only say after all the stories of Jews being hunted, herded, beaten, and killed across the centuries that I am of this community. And that this is a community that goes beyond Jews. History is a conflict between two tribes: one that hunts and one that welcomes. I am of the welcoming tribe. And after all the stories, in all cultures, of those cornered, giving up, standing up, and fighting back, I can only say that we are one.

We must look at these atrocities because looking away only enables cruelty to grow like bacteria. And let no one judge any of those who lost their lives in Warsaw or Prague. No matter how difficult, we must honor all the responses of those who died, so we can understand what refuses to die in each of us. Whether they took their own lives or were frightened into a ditch or fought till the end, no one knows what is possible or necessary until we ourselves are on that edge. We must accept that we are capable of being torn like a flower or standing our ground against all odds till the last.

I only know that under all wounds, we feel the same loss. Under all surrender, we seek the same joy. Under all languages, we need the same trust. Perhaps, because of these stories, I will be kinder without knowing it.

Forget the hours of suffering,
but not what they have taught you.

QUESTIONS TO WALK WITH

- In your journal, tell the story of a time when you were faced with standing up for who you are. What was the benefit and cost of being so visible?

- In conversation with a friend or loved one, take turns describing your ancestry and what you owe to your ancestors.

10

STUDENT-SELF AND TEACHER-SOUL

IN A CONVERSATION with a student, the Hindu sage Ramana Maharshi was asked, "While searching for the God within, should we keep part of our attention on the physical work at hand?"

Sri Ramana spoke softly, "The Self is Universal. So all actions will go on whether you strain yourself to be engaged in them or not. The work will go on by itself. . . . It's not for [us] to work and worry about it . . . but to allow [our deeper] nature to carry out the will of a Higher Power."

"But," the student replied, "the work may suffer if I don't attend it."

Sri Ramana answered clearly, "Attending to the Self *means* attending to the work."

What are we to make of this exchange? When Sri Ramana speaks of the need to attend "the Self," he's referring to the center we carry that is larger than our identity and older than our personal history. He's referring to the Hindu notion of namaste, which means "I bow to the piece of God, the piece of the Universe that resides in you." When we attend to the piece of God we carry within, we attend to the work and the work goes on by itself.

To understand this fully, we need to look at the assumptions of both the student and the teacher. Inherent in the student's question is the assumption that inner work and outer work are separate realities. And so his earnest question is one of time management. How can we attend two important things at once? The student is looking for an answer of technique: how to do this better.

But inherent in his teacher's answer is the assumption that these two essential forms of life-work are actually the same. And so his teacher's counsel is that attending one is attending both. Like a twin-trunked tree that has a common root, watering one is watering both; pruning one is pruning both.

The student resists this counsel, and Sri Ramana says only what he knows to be true: that attending to "the Self" *is* attending to the work. The Universe resides *in* the work. Through the work of being here, we find the God within. Sri Ramana offers this truth not as a viewpoint but as the acknowledgment of a spiritual condition that exists beyond debate, like gravity.

So the student within us is looking for time-management skills, while the teacher within us is offering a different way of apprehending reality.

This essential difference between what we ask of our soul and what our soul gives in return reveals some recurring choices in our very human struggle to stay authentic. Before we look at these, let me affirm that we each have both of these voices living within us: the voice of the student always asking for better techniques of how to manage what life presents, and the voice of the wise teacher who once asked will tend not to give us what we ask for, but rather offer us a different way of apprehending reality, which, if we dare to try, will often soften or eliminate the problem at the heart of our asking.

This doesn't mean there aren't problems to solve, but whether we approach our problems from a grasp of the Whole or serve the tensions and urgency of our problems determines the kind of choices we make. It's important to acknowledge that both the student-self and the teacher-soul are essential to our life on Earth. Without our student-self managing our ride through existence, we wouldn't be able to survive in the world. And without our teacher-soul calling us into the wonders of being alive, survival becomes pointless.

Let's look at these inner voices more closely. When faced with a problem, we always have this initial choice: whether to listen to our inner teacher or to stubbornly adhere to the condition of our problem. This choice centers on a very personal and repeatable practice of whether we give energy to the stream of life that carries our problem, or to our fear growing from the circumstance we're in. For each time our student-self insists on believing that the inner and outer life are separate realities, we deepen our tension and doubt. And each time we dare to surrender and listen to our inner teacher and stretch the way we take things in, we deepen our resilience and faith in life.

When we feel the press of the world intensify, we have this second choice: to try to hold it all together by managing it better or to look below the press of our circumstance in order to apprehend where things are strained but still connected. From the Oneness of Things, we can better discern the precise effort that will help us move more cleanly through the problem.

Very often, our anxious self will attack a problem, looking for how to juggle, maintain, or solve what has been set in motion, while the teacher within will stand back and question our very assumptions, even our very definition of what constitutes a problem. When we can endure the disorientation and discomfort that our inner teacher opens us to, we can step, however awkwardly, into greater authenticity.

So how do we endure the disorientation and discomfort necessary to apprehend reality differently? This depends on whether we stay willful or risk our surrender. This presents a third choice: whether to dig in and keep asserting our will, trying to obliterate the problem, or whether to surrender and drop down into a deeper apprehension of things. Often, if we can surrender into that deeper sense of things, we become aware of larger patterns, which often present the one clear action that makes inner sense.

Often, surrender is misconstrued as abdicating all action, when it is more about leaning into the currents of the powers that surround us and our problem—the way a Native American will hold his wet finger in the air to see which way the wind is blowing before sending smoke signals.

It is the vigilance of our student-self that wants to protect us from life, while our teacher-soul knows that the best protection is to submerge our problem into the river of life. It's our fear of randomness that has us overmanage risk, while our soul shows us repeatedly how to risk finding the current that will carry us. Ultimately, when we can drop into a deeper apprehension of things, problems are undone more than solved. When so alive and engaged, being human is the fifth element.

The student within us is looking for time-management skills, while the teacher within us is offering a different way of apprehending reality.

Questions to Walk With

- In this meditation, center yourself and breathe slowly. With each breath, try to drift below whatever circumstance or problem you're preoccupied with. Inhale slowly and know that this moment you're entering doesn't need to be solved or managed. With each breath, open yourself to the deeper part of your being that is content to have you simply keep it company. With each breath, try to see the world, your problems, your very life, with the eyes of your teacher-soul. During your day, try to view problems and preoccupations from this deeper perspective. Notice any shift in the tensions you carry.

- In your journal, use a recent problem you have faced or are facing to explore a personal case study of your conversation between your student-self and teacher-soul. There is no right or wrong way to enter this. Ask yourself these questions: Are you seeing the problem with the eyes of your inner teacher, or are you stubbornly adhering to the condition of your problem? Are you trying to hold it all together, or are you trying to apprehend where things are strained but still connected? And are you trying to assert your will, or are you trying to understand the deeper currents of the stream of life of which you are a part?

11

Original Steps

A bull contents himself with one meadow, and one forest
is enough for a thousand elephants; but the little body of
man devours more than all other living creatures.

—Seneca the Younger

Our concern about nature and the environment has ancient roots. For we have always struggled between using up the
Earth and honoring it. In the aftermath of the Iraqi war, many
artifacts were unearthed, including a clay tablet discovered
in the Kurdistan region of Iraq, which has added twenty lines
to *The Epic of Gilgamesh,* one of the oldest narratives known
to humanity. The twelve original Assyrian tablets date back to
2000 B.C. The newly found tablet was acquired from looters by
the Sulaymaniyah Museum for $800.

The story of Gilgamesh centers on an enervated and self-
centered king who declares war against the nature deity, Humbaba, in hopes of securing eternal fame. Into this war, he drags
his only friend, Enkidu.

The newly discovered lines to the epic reveal a sense of guilt and remorse in Enkidu for having killed the nature deity and for having decimated the Cedar Forest, the home of Humbaba. Enkidu says, "We have reduced the forest [to] a wasteland." His anxiety about offending the gods has Enkidu imagine an angry god, Enlil, asking Enkidu and Gilgmaesh when they arrive home, "What was this wrath of yours that you went trampling the forest?"

It's timely that this story should surface in our modern world. For this question from our better angels has been ringing in our ears for centuries and is even more pertinent today. What is the source of the wrath that we fester and carry that enables us to trample the forest, the planet, and each other—again and again?

In truth, our ecological problems are evidence of a deeper, spiritual problem whereby we keep shrinking our circle of compassion; whereby we, feeling empty, use everything up in an attempt to fill ourselves; whereby we, feeling insignificant and ephemeral, mark up the Earth in order to feel important and lasting; whereby we, feeling incomplete, break apart anything that is whole.

Since the beginning of the human trek through time, we've tried to silence our fear of death by puffing ourselves up and by making a lot of noise. When feeling less than, we've tried to hoard jewels and power. When desperate to feel, we've propagated violence for its shock and alarm.

Despite all this, each of us is born with a filament of being, which goes by many names. Essentially, under all our angst and stress, there's a pilot light of Spirit that we steward while here. Despite all the things we break, our filaments of being innately want to join. In this way, we're born to complete each other: each of us arriving with an inclination, a yearning for other life. This is a form of spiritual pollination, the inadvertent way that we long for the nectar of others and leave traces of the Spirit we steward wherever we love.

Those born in the deep pollinate the world with their depth. Those born in the world pollinate the introverted with the world. And those who cross both ways—bringing the deep and the worldly together—are ambassadors of Wholeness. Though we can be agitated into breaking and destroying, we're always a breath away from the innate pull of being and joining, of loving and completing each other. As the world comes alive each spring because of thousands of pollinations, there's a renaissance of care that blossoms in each generation from the spiritual pollination we are all born to partake of.

While there are infinite ways to stumble and do harm, the purpose of consciousness is to reduce the distance between who we are and what we do, between what we know and how we care.

We've always known that we must care for the Earth as we care for ourselves, though we've always turned away from this truth. In Denali National Park in Alaska, the permafrost, just below the surface, is a delicate fabric that holds the earth together. When trampled, the fabric that holds things together is broken. Therefore, in Denali, hikers are asked *not* to walk in the same place twice, *not* to form or follow a path. Instead of one following another, hikers are asked to walk side by side. In this way, without design or intention, a network of original steps is formed that keeps things together, rather than singular grooves that are deepened into ruts that will split things apart. In just this way, the life of a community depends on how we care for the ground we stand on and how we step lightly, walking side by side.

While there are infinite ways to stumble and do harm, the purpose of consciousness is to reduce the distance between who we are and what we do, between what we know and how we care.

QUESTIONS TO WALK WITH

- In your journal, describe a time when, feeling insignificant, you did something to try to feel important. Did this act alleviate your feeling of insignificance? Given the chance, how might you do this differently?

- In conversation with a friend or loved one, describe an instance in which you inadvertently helped pollinate the world.

12

DISTRIBUTING THE WEIGHT

Everybody's hurt. What is important, what corrals
you, what bullwhips you, what drives you, torments
you, is that you must find some way of using this to
connect you with everyone else alive. This is all you
have to do it with.

—JAMES BALDWIN

YOU AND I have talked for years, like fish mouthing pebbles along
the bottom for something small that might keep us going. And,
as often happens, I was moved by our conversation last night. I
understand how you feel the presence of suffering always in the
background, juxtaposed against the peaceful times and moments
of abundance we chance upon. I've felt this too and have come to
sense that we all take turns in these places, and that it does no good
for everyone to be suffering at once. When blessed to be well, we
balance the world by being conduits of light for the time being, as
long as we stay touchable.

The ever-present call of compassion is to widen our circle

and never close our hearts to those in need. This doesn't substitute for helping others in real time. But when unable to help, our commitment to feeling blessed when we *are* blessed adds light to the dark and distributes the weight of the world, as long as we let in the pain of others. When suffering myself, I've felt discarded by those who remain self-enclosed in their happiness, but I've also felt uplifted by the happiness of those who don't forget those who are hurting. Their tenderness arrives like the sun warming me in my painful places.

The plight of the less fortunate is always with me. This awareness led me to write this poem:

IN THE MILKY OCEAN

*As you pour milk on your cereal, I am
grateful for the sound of milk flowing over
dried grain, for the peace that lets us wake
and eat together, to stare at each other in
silence like small animals. I am aware how
safely tumbled through Eternity we are. Not
to be hunted from birth. Or chased into the
forest and forced to part. Or beaten for a
secret some warlord thinks we're hiding. I
eat my toast and close my eyes. How is it
we're alive in a place that has running water,
where milk and eggs are plentiful? Atrocities
and wonders flutter through me. They bleed
into each other. I can't stop it. The milk
tastes good as my twin is somewhere on
the run. It seems impossible to feel so
many fates at once. Impossible not to.*

Still, there are days I forget and days I'm too wrapped up in my own fear to remember the connection between us all. And when finally resting in the smallest inch of beauty, I can fear that letting your pain in will sink me back into my terrible darkness—as if we own the beauty and peace that move through us. On good days, I remember that we're called to let this borrowed inch of light pass on to someone else who has fallen back into the tangle of suffering we're all a part of. Inevitably, we're asked to be channels for what we're given, beyond our collapse into feeling small and dark.

When we can accept all that we're capable of, including the ways we can be insensitive and cruel, then we have a felt-basis for understanding and accepting the full humanity in everyone. This is the humble threshold to releasing our compassion. In this way, self-acceptance is the gateway to accepting the world, not accepting all that we do to each other, but believing in our inborn capacity, in spite of all we do, to repair what we do to each other.

It's taken me years to understand that wisdom waits in those who suffer. And since we all suffer, we all have a wisdom that is sorely needed. We each earn a view that the rest of us need. And yet we shy away from asking those in pain, "What has your pain opened?" From asking those near death, "From this great height, what do you see of life?" From asking those on the other side of fear, "What has all that trembling revealed?"

What we drop, others pick up. What we lose, others find. What we forget, others remember. What we love spreads like weeds. Our lives and all we go through seed a spring we'll never see.

I was changed by our conversation last night, because we

pulled aside our veils and came closer to the truth than ever before. Ultimately, we're here to suffer when we suffer, and to put down all we carry and accept joy when it comes, so we can balance out the weight of being here. This is the noble anonymity of care.

The ever-present call of compassion is to widen our circle and never close our hearts to those in need.

Questions to Walk With

- In your journal, describe a time you felt alone in your pain or grief because someone you know refused to let your pain or grief mix with their happiness. What did this do to the relationship?

- In conversation with a friend or loved one, discuss the challenge of being happy while you know others are suffering. Explore how to make room in your heart for both.

13

Our Walk in the World

EVERYONE BORN TO this life is challenged to survive and thrive. Yet if we survive without thriving, what's the point? When preoccupied with survival, we become pragmatists, pessimists, and even nihilists. When lost in the gears of existence, we're always challenged to let in beauty *while* we're suffering, to let in love *while* we're struggling. What holds everything together, what releases resilience, and what renews us when we're struggling is relationship. Relationship is the lifeblood of inner health.

But we are so battered at times by the tumult of survival that it sticks to us with its thick residue. And through that film, we can give rise to a nest of dark voices that will strangle our effort to be, voices of lack that can keep us from kissing the earth and lifting our face to the sun. When entangled this way, we can be misguided by the intensity of our fear and worry, by the piercing tones of regret and disappointment. Our vision can be discolored by the heavy veil of grief.

Feelings of fear, worry, regret, disappointment, and grief are natural, wise teachers unto themselves, only debilitating when we refuse to let the rest of life in. I know. For I have been discolored by fear and debilitated by grief and pierced by the loss of those I thought I could count on. Yet this is all part of the ride, part of the expansion and contraction of being human. This is part of our walk in the world. Inevitably, we're challenged to still our voices of lack, to calm the exaggeration of our fears, and to right-size our pain. This is a never-ending practice: to face the more difficult parts of our experience, which if unchecked will create havoc in our soul and therefore in the world.

Still, each time we're loved or broken open, what we keep tucked away merges with the ever-evolving world, making our heart expand till we are closer to things. After such moments, we're more integrated and less capable of tucking things away, as the inner world and the outer world—which are really one world—alchemize within us. It seems that storms are meant to break our habits, until forced open by experience and soothed by love, we have no choice but to become students of what it means to be alive.

Like all forms of life, we open and close constantly. In fact, we're so practiced in sorting what comes our way that we often miss the lessons that come from what the sum of our experiences say when allowed to gather inside us. Normally, we make love, sleep, have breakfast, go to the dentist, and drive home in the rain, and these events have nothing to do with each other. But the other day, I couldn't keep them separate, and they led me to see what a good man my dentist is, because I was able to look at him with my lover's eyes. It made me well up, realizing in that softened moment what a gift it is to feel at all.

Still, we're overrun by urgency. Like everyone, I've spent too much time responding to alarms and crises, many of which—

once on the scene—were not as urgent as they seemed. The truth is that unless someone is bleeding or can't breathe, there is no urgency. For sure, the things we face are significant, and there are endless problems, and the bend of unexpected circumstance never goes away. But while much is important, very little is urgent. Understanding this is the threshold to peace. For while surviving demands a great deal from us to get from day to day, being alive asks nothing of us. Stripped of our urgency, being alive is its own reward.

When in the hospital during my struggle with cancer, I lived with an underlying urgency that I couldn't find and couldn't let go of. In time, I realized that making every situation urgent was how I played cat and mouse with my fear of death. Finally, this constant sense of urgency exhausted me and I collapsed in the moment I was given. Then the moments I was given began to open around me. Once there, I began to drink from life.

Since then, I've learned that when urgent, we constrict and life crashes against us. When exhausted or loved into a sense of surrender, we expand and life flows through us. Being human, we will always become urgent and constrict, and then in time surrender and expand. No one can escape this. But it helps to know that being urgent is like having a cramp in your heart or mind. It will pass.

In fact, on the other side of great pain or exhaustion, we're often stalled enough to receive a strength of being from settling into things as they are. For underneath the turbulence of circumstance and the tide of emotion that comes from living, we're challenged to put down the press of urgency that comes from all directions, so we might discover the authority of being that connects all living things. When touched by that common well of Spirit, we're able to enter a stillness that lets us feel the foundation of existence under all our trouble.

Over the years, I've learned that the inner life is not a refuge in which to hide from experience, but a practice ground from which to gather strength and clarity to enter the world.

The task of coming alive and staying alive is beautiful and endless. Every day, we're asked to move at the pace of what is real, to take the risk to be wholehearted, and to have the courage to stay soft and strong and kind. These vows of authenticity allow us to thrive. In moments of thriving, we repair each other and illuminate the world.

While much is important, very little is urgent.
Understanding this is the threshold
to peace.

Questions to Walk With

- In your journal, begin a conversation between that in you which needs to survive and that in you which needs to thrive. How are these voices in you at odds with each other? How do they complement each other?

- In conversation with a friend or loved one, tell the story of an urgency you are currently carrying and discuss what urgency feels like for you. Is the urgency you currently feel in proportion to what is being asked of you?

OUR TRUE INHERITANCE

The waking have one common world, but the sleeping turn aside, each into a world of their own.

—Heraclitus

When we speak of being a spiritual warrior, a concept referred to in many traditions, we're describing a journey of transformation that is steadfast in its adherence to both love and truth in the face of the constant storms that life on Earth generates. The word "war" itself traces back to the Indo-European root wers, *which means "to confuse, mix up." War and the inevitable conflict it produces—both within us and between us—stem from a state of confusion. Thus, a spiritual warrior is one devoted to the clearing of confusion, both inwardly and out in the world. The word "veteran" refers to anyone having long experience or practice. It traces back to the Indo-European root* wet, *which means "to inspire or spiritually engage." These origins point to the relational call to carry our beasts of burden while staying engaged in an atmosphere of Spirit, until we clear all confusion and establish enduring roots. This is our true inheritance. This is the work of a spiritual warrior, a veteran of life, not just individually but in community. This work is indispensable and elusive, ours alone to do and impossible to do alone. Few things are more worthwhile to pursue. The chapters in this section speak to the ways we discover our true inheritance and the ways we share our burdens and clear our confusion.*

14

THE FIRE OF ALIVENESS

That law of life, so cruel and just, [which demands] that
one must grow or else pay more for remaining the same.
—NORMAN MAILER

In the Judaic tradition, heart is the crucible of a
person's true essence.
—GAIL GODWIN

THERE ARE TWO fires that we have to encounter daily. The first
is the fire of life, which reduces us to joy by burning away all
that is false and not essential. This is *the fire of aliveness* that
needs to be fed, no matter where we are or what we do. This is
the light of the soul that must be kept burning. The second is
the fire in the world, which can burn us up, which can wound
us and damage us. This is *the fire of circumstance* that needs to
be put out. How do we know the difference between these two
fires? I don't know. I've been reduced to what is essential by the

one and wounded by the flames of the other, more than once. Nevertheless, we need each other to know which fire to feed and which to douse, if we are to clear our confusions and establish enduring roots. Helping each other know the difference is part of the work of love.

Though we rightfully feel the rip and pull of everything taken away from us, being stripped of what covers us helps us grow—by lightening our load and making us more raw and naked, so we can be touched and transformed by the elements of life. This seems to be the promise of the inner world—that if we stay open to life, we'll be cleansed of dead weight, worn of coverings that have served their purpose, and pruned of the tangle of falseness that grows like vines about everything.

Inevitably, we move through the first half of life gathering, only to enter the second half of life compelled to empty much of what we carry. Along the way, we gather knowledge, achieve a great deal, and save what we can. But under all our coverings, we long for the naked freedom of a star. Under all our accomplishments is a simple soul eager to build, not caring what it is we might build. And stripped of what we save and hoard, we grow immediate. This cycle continues: gather, build, grow covered by what we build, then burn away all that is not essential, so we can grow immediate, ready to build again.

In these raw, essential moments, we're left with a life that has to live now, eager as a fish gulping for food at the surface. By gathering, we *discover* who we are, and by emptying, we get to throw off the world and *be* who we are. From such bareness of being, we enter a simple and substantial experience of life.

This brings us to a more compelling definition of destiny.

Destiny is not a particular dream coming true over time for an individual, but the force of Spirit emanating into the world through all things, including us. The emanation of Spirit is the counterpart to gravity. Like flowers that break ground in order to blossom, human beings are destined to bring their souls into the world. And despite the thousand things that can deter us, this can happen in a thousand and one ways.

Our ordinary destiny, then, is to accept the friction of being worn open by the world, so our soul can show itself and join with everything. The sensation of our soul showing itself and joining with everything is another name for joy.

Yet how can we discern between life's fires when there are storms everywhere? It helps to stand still in the storm and listen for the truth, until we can hear voices more ancient and telling than our own. This takes a quiet fortitude. As the Danish philosopher Søren Kierkegaard (1813–1855) said:

> As my prayer became more attentive and inward, I had less and less to say. I finally became completely silent. . . . This is how it is. To pray does not mean to listen to oneself speaking. Prayer involves becoming silent, and being silent, and waiting until God is heard.

Listening this way, we can uncover what is true in the midst of that relentless and mysterious teacher, experience.

Still, living between the fire of aliveness and the fire of circumstance lands us in the middle of another paradox. While no one can live your life for you, we're woefully deficient in the wisdom necessary to live, if left to our experience alone. Just as we can't see unless our eyes are open, we need the experience and company of others to open our deeper mind, though we're left to do the seeing for ourselves.

Though we'd rather be open than closed, we're constantly challenged to work with both. We're given both because our call in being human is to reveal who we are by opening and closing repeatedly, just as we wake and sleep day after day. But how do we bear the tenderness after being loved or broken open? There are as many answers as lives.

If too open, we can become wounded and burdened. If too closed, we can become removed and untouchable. Most of the time, we tumble in the space in between. This is where we live, risking our way into authentic engagement, not watching life go by, but not burning up in the fire of circumstance, either. How? Who knows? This is the tension that everyone faces sooner or later: how to be touched by life without being consumed by its fire.

Throughout the ages, those damaged by the fire of circumstance early in their lives tend to see life as a fire to be put out. While those enlivened by the fire of aliveness early on tend to see life as a fire to be lit. Often, these two will find each other—as lovers, friends, or colleagues—in order to challenge each other, to balance each other, and to complete each other. In time, the spiritual journey invites us to understand the powerful nature of both fires.

When Hannah and Edward met after World War II, they fell deeply in love, though their life journeys were vastly different. Hannah was a child of the Holocaust, her consciousness charred by heinous acts no child should ever have to see. Hannah had been burned by the fire of circumstance so early in life that she believed the world unsafe. She anticipated fires everywhere. Edward was the son of a railroad tycoon. He grew up in Philadelphia, shielded for the most part from the hardships of life. He was introduced to the fire of aliveness through music and science and the deeper inquiry waiting beneath all circumstance. Though bad things happened, he felt the world was inherently safe.

Hannah and Edward recognized the same depth in each other, though they'd been introduced to it differently. Their love was strong. As the years went on and life continued to surprise them, they would argue about whether life was safe or not, good or bad, just or random. But each secretly depended on the other's stance to balance their own. Like X and Y chromosomes, Hannah and Edward had joined as atoms of the two fires. Together, they formed a vibrant cell of life trying to stay alive.

The very sensitivity that can save us can also throw us under. The gifted poet Sylvia Plath took her life in 1963 at the age of thirty. She was depressed for sure, but more, she appears to have been one of those born with a godlike sensitivity that she couldn't turn off, unable to escape the fire of circumstance and unable to fully feed the fire of her aliveness. Plath can be seen as a modern John Keats, a precocious being silenced before her full wisdom could be voiced.

The poet Ted Hughes was married to Plath, and sadly, in 2009, their son Nicholas hung himself. In a letter to Nicholas months before, his father wrote:

> *That's how we measure our real respect for people—by the degree of feeling they can register, the voltage of life they can carry and tolerate—and enjoy.*

In this deep remark, I feel how the widower and powerless father was trying to honor the power in the fire of aliveness and the danger in the fire of circumstance, trying to warn his sensitive son of the fine line between the charge and pain inherent in the voltage of life. But we each must stand alone between the two fires and find our way.

Vincent van Gogh is another poignant example of someone born with a godlike sensitivity, whose fire of aliveness roared through him into his paintings, while the same sensitivity allowed him to be consumed by the fire of circumstance. We each experience our own degree of godlike sensitivity, and one of life's initiations is to learn how to make a resource of our sensitivity without shutting it down, how to use our sensitivity to get strength from what we know.

It's humbling but true: we live between the kindling of dream and the fire of life. Confused, we often think the dream is where we're going, and so miss the majesty of what the dream ignites. As Keats advised, we need beauty and truth to make it through life. And I would add love. Truth will help us douse the fire of circumstance when it sears us with its flames, and beauty, the way of seeing that rises from love, will help us keep the fire of aliveness from going out.

This is the tension that everyone faces sooner or later: how to be touched by life without being consumed by its fire.

QUESTIONS TO WALK WITH

- In your journal, describe one effort of gathering, building, or saving in your life and how that has helped you discover who you are. Then describe one effort of emptying, uncovering, or giving away in your life and how that has helped you be who you are.

- In conversation with a friend or loved one, describe a time when you fed the fire of your aliveness and how this kept you vital. Then describe a time when you put out the fire of circumstance and how this lessened some fear or pain. Finally, discuss how you experience the difference between the fire of aliveness and the fire of circumstance.

15

The Slowing of the Land

> There is a day
> when the road neither
> comes nor goes, and the way
> is not a way but a place.
> —Wendell Berry

I DIDN'T WANT to go. But here we are, driving to Bangor. We take a right at the blinking yellow light, another right on Hastings Court, and then down a dirt road to Blue Dog Greens. Twenty-eight acres of agreeable land tucked between the railroad tracks and Black River. Dennis and Shawna live here, very simply, in order to tend this organic farm. It's a sunny, windblown day in July, and close to thirty of us show up to help harvest the garlic. About an acre to pull up, shake off, carry, rope, and hang in the rafters of the open-air shed, high enough that the animals can't nibble at the cloves.

After a few rows, I get the hang of it: pull the stalk up directly so the garlic won't break off underground. Some come easily, as if waiting for us to finally bring them like a birth into the world. Others hold back, as if saying "We're not ready; leave us be." Either way there's a small tug before the roots break free. I pull up fifty or so and stop to stretch my back, when I hear the wind bending the oaks and maples at the edge of the field. I can see the bunch of us scattered through the beds, bending and pulling in the rows. Something wells up in me. For a moment, I feel part of some unannounced community that has come together throughout time: showing up to harvest, to pull what we can from the ground, to dry it out and wait, so it can feed the lot of us when the ground freezes and things seem rough.

This is such hard work, not pulling up the garlic, but the slowing of the land till it yields something edible and sustainable. And though we think of bounty when we think of harvest, the process is much more complex and telling, endemic of resiliency on Earth. The land is broken of its grip so it can receive a seed, then watered till the seed can take root, then covered and protected from birds and rabbits and raccoons, then weeded to keep the other wild things from suffocating what is slowly growing. And finally, when the edible thing has grown its own roots, we come along and tear those roots so it can feed us.

This is not harsh but intimately natural, only callous when we forget what harvest means. Only wasted when we don't make the connection to how this process works in our own lives—how everything we love and want requires this slowing, until what matters takes hold of us, enough that we will break its roots so it can feed us.

Some come easily, as if waiting for us to finally bring them like a birth into the world.

QUESTIONS TO WALK WITH

- In your journal, describe the process of one thing that has taken root in you over time. What does this process tell you about the nature of living?

- Go with a friend or loved one and participate in some kind of harvesting. Later, discuss what this experience was like for each of you. Describe one aspect of harvesting that can be applied to the inner harvest we call maturing.

16

STAYING POSSIBLE

I test the limits of myself in order to transform
myself, but I also take the energy from the audience
and transform it. It goes back to them in a different
way. . . . A powerful performance will transform
everyone in the room.

—MARINA ABRAMOVIĆ

ONE WOMAN CAME all the way from Australia to sit before
her and look in her eyes. Another young woman stood before her and slipped out of her dress. Later, in tears, she said
she only wanted to meet Marina's vulnerability with her own.
Another quiet, burdened man sat before her in silence for an
entire day, as others, waiting their turn, grew angry and restless.
Altogether, Marina Abramović sat in silence on a wooden chair
within a circle of light in the atrium of the Museum of Modern Art (MOMA) for 632 hours. For eight hours a day, from
March 14 through May 31, 2010, the tenaciously gentle artist

openly welcomed anyone to sit in a single chair opposite her, to sit and look in silence into each other's eyes for as long as each wanted. Such a fundamental inspiration: to give all our presence and attention in order to see and accept the heart within a stranger until the strangeness evaporates. Such a quiet giving: to seed that presence in the world.

As the days progressed, the gravity of the openness she'd convened grew stronger and lines formed outside the museum. Some would sit for a minute, some much longer. Every day, several would break open to their tears. With each day, the crowd deepened, thickened, and the place of true meeting between two beings in two chairs kept rippling into the crowd. This living exhibit, called *The Artist Is Present*, was part of a retrospective of Marina's life's work.

In her mid-seventies, Marina Abramović is a legendary performance artist whose canvas has been reality and whose paintings are events that have evoked the raw and complex connections that bond and tangle human beings together, no matter how we try to isolate ourselves. For more than four decades, she has bravely used her body and being as the living litmus by which to expose and score the ways we brutalize each other and care for each other. In these honest experiments, she has revealed the dangers and gifts of what it means to be in community. She has made visible the violence of our failures and the love inherent in our successes.

The Artist Is Present broke attendance records at MOMA, drawing more than half a million participants, with 1,400 people sitting in the chair. During the last month, she removed the table between the two chairs and everything became more direct, more immediate, more vulnerable. Sitting still for so long was extremely difficult. Choosing a chair without arms turned out to be a mistake. "This one detail made it hellish," she said, "The shoulders sag, the arms swell, the pain starts to increase. Then the ribs are going into the organs. I had an incredible amount of physical pain and even some out-of-body experiences where the pain just vanishes, but always it comes back."

Abramović was born in Belgrade in what was Yugoslavia in 1946, the daughter of strict, military heroes who had prominent positions in Tito's postwar government. "When people ask me where I am from," she says, "I never say Serbia. I always say I come from a country that no longer exists." As happens throughout history, a war-torn land produces a global, timeless citizen whose voice belongs to no one but speaks for everyone.

As the days unfolded in the atrium at MOMA, you could see Marina's face relax. You could see her heart take over her body. You could see her already deep eyes deepen to a place below her identity and given name. I recognize this place as the kiss of Eternity that almost took me when I had cancer, but which somehow buoyed me back into life with a rawness of heart by which I know everyone before we meet. Marina's face seemed to open in the same way. As she let soul after soul pour their pain and love in the sudden, safe place between the two wooden chairs, this quiet, soft spot in the middle of the city began to feel holy.

Through her unmitigated presence, Marina Abramović drew the possibility and aliveness of everyone who sat before her into the open. Quickly, the exchange of aliveness began to spark and happen, like wind on water or sunlight spreading over sleeping plants. The aliveness began to arc between people who for the moment remembered they are alive. What else can we ask of each other?

Marina was honest in her stillness, completely bare and transparent, offering nothing extraneous, holding nothing back. She sat in complete stillness for more than six hundred hours, like a flower slowly opening around its eternal eye. Authentic beings confirm for me that the atom of community is more about complete presence than achievement, more about the exchange of aliveness than any ounce of genius worked into gold.

In Naples in 1974, Marina convened one of her most dangerous and telling events, *Rhythm O*. For six hours she stood passively, surrounded by seventy-two instruments she had gathered. Some objects could give pleasure, while others could inflict pain. They included a rose, a feather, honey, a whip, scissors, a scalpel, matches, lipstick, saws, nails, and even a gun with a single bullet in its chamber. Visitors were invited to do whatever they desired to her. This daring convening opened the impulsive darkness that each of us is capable of. Some people became vicious: marking, probing, scratching her, blindfolding her, dousing her with cold water, pinning slogans to her skin. One person tried to rape her, another stopped him. All the while, Marina completely received whatever was brought to her. After six hours, she moved for the first time and walked toward the audience, and everyone ran away. Later she confessed, "Because of this performance, I know where to draw the line so as not to put myself at such risk." Her experiment magnified the quandary for us all: While being vulnerable and accepting is the key to all connection, how long do we stay open in the presence of the unawakened?

Now, all these years later, the artist seems to be saying, we need to stay open to everything longer than is comfortable or nothing lasting will happen. Repeatedly, this woman, born in a country that no longer exists, has offered her complete presence to exorcise the violence she was born into. In truth, this gentle, ferocious worker of reality appears before us as a female counterpart of Hephaestus, the ancient Greek blacksmith born of the gods but not a god—Hephaestus, the lame master craftsman who hammered and forged the tools and armor for the gods. And after a lifetime of probing and forging, Marina simply sat in the open, as an artist who paints with reality, to say without saying, *Let's go back to the beginning and sit in silence and look into each other's eyes until the place from which we all spring shows itself and we can know each other again.*

In each of those souls who sat with Marina during those seventy-nine days, a seed of true meeting was awakened. And no matter where they are or what they are doing now, together they opened a long moment of community. Through their mutual presence, they formed one organism of humanity. That awakening of mutual presence is the seed of our human kinship that can germinate anywhere.

In each generation, alone and together, we have this repeatable chance to stay possible. It is a birthright we often put down or tuck away, the chance to enliven ourselves to the fullest and thereby spark an exchange of aliveness that illuminates the gifts of humanity. Under all the proposals and reformations, it is the covenant of being fully present that lets us see where we are joined. It is as simple and brave as sitting in silence on two chairs facing each other—until the soft truth rises out of us, making our care useful. When we can stop and let our souls rest in our being, without hiding, we can find the one kinship living in each other's eyes.

Such a fundamental inspiration: to give all our presence and attention in order to see and accept the heart within a stranger until the strangeness evaporates.

QUESTIONS TO WALK WITH

- Sit opposite a friend or loved one in silence and simply look into each other's eyes for as long as it takes to soften before each other, until the opened moment passes. Take a deep breath and then listen to each other describe what opened within you and between you.

17

LESSENING FEAR

> A person who is beginning to sense the suffering
> of life is, at the same time, beginning to awaken to
> deeper realities. . . . For suffering smashes to pieces
> the complacency of our normal fictions about reality,
> and forces us to become alive in a special sense—to
> see carefully, to feel deeply, to touch ourselves and our
> worlds in ways we have avoided.
>
> —KEN WILBER

FROM THE MOMENT we're born, we begin to leave. From our first breath, we enter a lifelong conversation with presence and absence, with awe and fear, with life and death. From the first blink of our eyes, we grow and shed at the same time. The prospect of wearing away and not living is alarming, and so it's natural to recoil from it. However, the more we pull away from what we fear, the stronger that fear becomes.

For much of our life, we bounce between our experience of wonder and impermanence. Along the way, we're asked to keep leaning in after pulling back, because we need the wonder of life and the impermanence of life to inform each other, to illuminate each other, to balance and right-size each other. The wonder lifts us and the impermanence grounds us. Without wonder, we become oppressed. Without impermanence, we're barely tethered. All the while, this basic paradox is unavoidable—that the spirit we carry is indestructible, though the container that we are will in time crumble. The very paradox of our existence underlies all other forms of fear.

In addition to this existential awareness, each person is born into a particular context. When blessed to arrive with enough food, shelter, and care, our first understanding of the world is that it is primarily safe. Awakened to this sense of safety, our natural resting position is one of accord with the Universe. When we stop, close our eyes, and enter silence, the still point we return to is calm and everlasting.

But when born without enough food, shelter, or care, we develop a primal understanding that the world is dangerous and not to be trusted. When we experience threat, violence, or abuse, we are forever on guard. The natural resting position here is not restful at all, but one of threat and anxiety. When burdened, we close our eyes and enter silence, often unable to find a still point to return to, and often left with the agitation and mistrust of a chaotic Universe. Yet depending on what happens to us, our sense of the Universe as safe or threatening can change.

On top of our existential fear of dying, and the safety or threat we're born into, we are always confronted with the most immediate appearance of fear in our lives, which is situational. I knock the hot kettle off the stove and have a rush of fear that

I will be burned. I come home for lunch to find my wife in bed and have a rush of fear that she might be ill. Or I lose my job and have a rush of fear about paying the mortgage.

These three continuums of fear have to be met, if we're to know any peace during our life. Underneath the situations we face, we're challenged to expand the nature of our resting position in life. Whatever situation we face or however we've been traumatized, there is a still point that exists beneath our personality. And that still point, that resting place—which all meditation practices aim to open—is where we can continue our fundamental conversation with the wonder of being alive and the prospect of dying.

Our primal conversation with living and dying is a central root in the tree of our life. The context we live into determines how our trunk will grow. And each situation we face challenges us to grow toward the light. But if our roots aren't strong, the tree of our life, with all its branches, won't survive to grow. This is why we must stay in our root conversation with life— engaging the mystery and miracle of being here, knowing we will eventually die.

Though no one knows how to do this, we're asked to absorb the prospect of not being here in order to inhabit the gift of being here. This requires a quiet, ongoing courage that will, in time, lessen the degree of fear in all other aspects of our life.

During my cancer journey, I learned a great deal about fear. When first diagnosed, I was terrified by every poke, prod, injection, and conversation with the sober doctors who didn't know what was going on inside my body. Within months, my fear of everything exhausted me. I was forced to discern among the many sensations that were overwhelming me, both physical and emotional. I began to realize that the first way to lessen my fear was to look more closely at it, so I could locate and inhabit the spaces in my fear. In the same way that quantum physicists look into the spaces between particles or that monks meditate until they descend into the spaces between their runaway thoughts, there are waves of stillness and peace that wait in the spaces of our agitations and fear.

Over the years, I've discovered that when I can stay open beyond my likes and dislikes, and stay devoted to a practice of gratitude, and take the risk to be tender, the habits of my fear unravel.

When obeying our fear, we begin to seek sameness and shun difference. The assumption that safety resides in seeking sameness is insidious throughout our culture. For example, while I marvel at the technology behind the music app Pandora, I disagree with its fundamental premise. Pandora is designed to only bring you music that is similar to what you already like. It hones the world of music to what is already preferred. I'm not singling out Pandora, just using it as an example of the difference between seeking experiences and people that will only confirm what we already know, and seeking experiences and people that will grow us and complete us because they are beyond what we already know. For welcoming experience beyond our likes and dislikes is what keeps us in conversation with life.

The same assumption feeds the industry of movie and theater reviews. It's fine to have discussion and evaluation around the merits of films and plays. But if we only expose ourselves to what others deem as good, we're basically courting sameness and missing the basic wonder of anything new. Whether I like a film or a play or a song matters less than the fact that I'm being nourished by new forms of life. I can dislike a movie and still be nourished by it.

One way to lessen our fear is to let in anything new *while* we're afraid. So if you're having a bad day and can't shake your anxiety, go see a bad movie or attend a strange play. Ignore the reviews and listen to music you've never heard of, even if it sounds odd. Don't let your likes and dislikes limit your exposure to the full spectrum of life, because it's the full spectrum of life that is healing. Being a cancer survivor, I can tell you that there is no bad weather. The only bad weather is no weather.

Staying devoted to a practice of gratitude is another way to lessen our fears. Gratitude is the way we meet life with nothing in the way. Since no one can do this constantly, gratitude is a tender opening and closing to the life before us. When grateful, even for the difficult passages that open us, we are closest to life itself.

Every day I'm grateful for just being here. At unexpected times, I'm returned to a gratitude for simple things: the innocent stare of my dog in the morning, the quiet breathing of my wife as she sleeps, the creep of morning light up the side of the house as the coffee drips, the mystery in how every person carries an unchartered world within them. Of course, I grow weary like everyone else, but it's gratitude that refreshes me. I often follow the feeling of gratitude, not sure what I'm grateful for. And that deep and simple feeling that arises from direct living becomes my teacher, opening the bare isness of things, which no one can destroy. Gratitude is how the heart opens our inner eye to the majesty of life. Gratitude returns us to the still point that exists beneath our personality.

Taking the risk to be tender can also lessen our fear. Everyone has a tenderness that waits in the center of their hardness, the way the softness of an oyster waits in its shell as it settles in the deep. When hurt, we believe the point of life is to protect that tender spot at all cost, to never expose it to an uncaring world. But against our will and in spite of our fear, we can discover, in a moment when we drop all that we carry, that it feels quite wonderful to carry nothing. Then we might wonder why we should pick it all up. Then we might be lifted by a sudden revelation that it's the other way around. We need to pry ourselves open and let the tenderness we were born with meet the world. We must risk being tender if we want to truly live.

Tenderness keeps us from running away. It opens us more deeply to where we are. Staying tender allows us to permeate hardship. When young, I'd feel afraid when poked with the wonder of being alive, and an urgency would overcome me to get up and run, to go somewhere I'd never been, to climb a mountain for the view or sit by a river I'd never seen. But now, when feeling afraid and poked by the ache of being alive, I move deeper into where I am. Now I try to part the moment like a wave and swim with my heart into the center of where I am, into the vibrant shimmering center that informs all moments everywhere. By staying tender, life has become a practice of opening what's before me rather than running to where I imagine life is easier.

Yet no matter how tender or grateful we are, each of us will be broken open at some point in our life. Though this will intensify our fear, how we meet being broken open begins a deeper phase of our spiritual journey. For against our will, we're made vulnerable and now the light we've carried within since birth can find its way into the world. At the same time, the light of the world can now enter us through a break in our shell, which we wouldn't have opened willingly. Now the light of the soul and the light of the world merge, becoming one. Now it's impossible to tell where the soul ends and the world begins, impossible to tell where you end and I begin. And so the heart is released into its flow of compassion.

In spite of our fear, in spite of whether we feel safe or threatened, when we love one thing, we begin to love everything. For love is not confined to what we love, any more than light is confined to the first thing it illuminates. When loving you, I learn to love the world. And seeing the truth in one thing, I begin to see the truth in everything. When facing my own stumblings, I learn to have compassion for the flawed beauty of humanity. When dipping my face in a pond, I honor the life of water that covers the Earth. When touched by the sweep of one chord in one concerto, I am touched by the river of music. When in awe at the workings of Einstein's mind, I learn how to appreciate all I don't know. And when feeling the devotion of someone praying to a face of God I don't understand, I acknowledge that we are all on the same journey. All these engagements with life lessen our fear.

Sometimes courage is not defending what we know to be true, but letting in all that is beyond our understanding. Our trust in life returns when we can stay in conversation with the larger flow of wonder and impermanence in which our life swims.

Gratitude returns us to the still point that exists beneath our personality.

QUESTIONS TO WALK WITH

- In your journal, enter your root conversation with life—engaging the mystery and miracle of being here, knowing we will eventually die. Try to stay with this conversation below the initial fear it engenders and listen for the still point beneath your personality and what it has to say to you.

- When feeling afraid, try letting in something new, or being grateful for something simple, or being tender toward yourself or someone you love. Later, in conversation with a friend or loved one, discuss if and how any of these gestures might have lessened your fear.

18

What to Bring Forward

What is the unseen relational piece to this situation?
—Cathy McNally

If you can understand any one thing deeply, it will
open you to a better understanding of everything.
—Mathematician Edward Burger

Each of the great sages and prophets was born with a weight
of expectation laid out before them—including Buddha, Jesus,
Moses, Muhammad, Gandhi, Krishnamurti, Martin Luther
King, Jr., and Nelson Mandela. And each refused what others
had prepared for them, because of their allegiance to a greater
inheritance that they directly intuited.

It takes courage to settle below all that's expected of us so
we can finally touch into what is innately ours. This doesn't
mean we can't learn from others or that there aren't traditions
worth carrying forward. But settling below all we've been

taught, below all that's planned for us, allows us to touch life directly without undue influence. From that direct knowing, we can choose authentically what to bring forward because it genuinely speaks to us, rather than what rises out of reflex or obligation. This is being faithful to our true inheritance.

The wisdom in being alive appears like sheet music. It can't be heard until played by each of us. It means rubbing our questions like bows against the strings of time. We learn by listening, reflecting, expressing, and relating to life directly. We learn from each other by asking to hear each other's song.

Knowing that you must sort out what is true for you, and knowing that you also need the wisdom of others to make your way, how will you build a bridge by which to cross the stream of trouble?

In building your own bridge to meaning, you will need your concern. Where is your concern? When was the last time you felt deep concern? Can you summon that concern within you now? You will also need that in you which can withstand the expectations of others. When was the last time you succumbed to a path that wasn't true for you? When was the last time you followed what you knew to be true in your heart? Can you discern the difference between following others and following your heart? You will need steps to your bridge, steps such as trust, wonder, care, and honesty.

So in the days to come, can you identify some part of life you have trust in? Can you identify some part of life you feel wonder about? Can you identify something you care about? And can you identify some part of life you need to be more honest about?

When we seek guidance in how to exhibit confidence or

to impress others, we're often instructed in how to carry ourselves. But the deeper question—"How do you carry what is essentially true?"—is much more profound. How do you carry your one soul, your one pilot light, so it might illumine all you touch and not go out? What will you feed your true self? How will you care for it?

In Swahili, the word *luglio* means "food that you carry with you." And in Latin, *viaticum,* a term for the Eucharist offered as Communion in the Catholic Church, means "food along the way." Both can refer to actual food, but they imply a deeper sort of food that can sustain the soul on its journey.

So how do you carry your one, essential self through the world? And what is the food that you carry on the way that sustains your soul's journey? No one can answer this for you. We each must define what will sustain us inwardly.

The word "manna" has a long history. During the forty years that the Jews wandered the desert after leaving their bondage in Egypt, manna was the name they gave the bread that mysteriously appeared to feed them, which would only stay fresh for one day. Later, when Jesus said, "Give us this day our daily bread," he invoked a renewable form of sustenance. In this regard, manna implies a form of spiritual nourishment that has to be remade every day.

In the Polynesian tradition, the early tribal peoples used the word *mana* to refer to the numinous spirit that informs everything, the glow of being that emanates from trees, rocks, rivers, fire, people, and from the spirits of ancestors now gone. Carl Jung added his own psychospiritual definition, when he described mana as the unconscious influence of one being on another.

Together, these definitions suggest that we carry a piece of the Universe within us like a little sun. Some call this our soul. When we can be completely who we are, the piece of the Universe we carry within emanates warmth and light in all directions without preference. When this authentic, we grow toward each other. Essentially, manna/mana, in all its accumulated meaning, represents the inner light we need in order to survive and grow. How do we personalize this inner light and eat and drink from it in a daily way?

Yet, though we need to make our daily bread, what matters takes time to show itself and rise. Like it or not, we're all required to be in relationship with the silent god of patience. Without the hard lessons of patience, we often make choices and decisions prematurely.

Outwardly, there's always the need to gather information in order to know what is possible. This is called research. But more important is our need for *insearch,* the time needed to know what is true in the deepest context. We need to wait for the fog in our head to clear. We need to wait for the turbulence in our heart to settle. We need time to truly see what's before us. The god of patience is a difficult ally who always sends uncertainty to interview us first, before coming to our aid.

I'm reminded of two sailors who were shipwrecked on a small island. After the shock wore off, they began to imagine life from this point on. Charlie was inclined to do only what was necessary to survive. Otherwise, he simply waited. Danny, his shipwrecked mate, asked him, "What are you waiting for? No one is coming." Charlie thought for a while and replied, "I'm just waiting. I'm not going to do anything meaningless anymore."

Danny shook his head and went about the island looking

for sharp stones to use as tools, and fallen trees to build with. As he dumped what he was gathering, Charlie asked him, "What are you doing?" Danny said, "This is how I wait, by building."

The two lost at sea represent our being and our doing, and how they often argue with each other; though we need both to make sense of where we land. The conversation between our being and doing can only unfold over time.

Under our being and doing, we have a quartet of competing voices. We have a voice in us that sees nothing. Everywhere we go, it keeps insisting that nothing matters. We have another voice that's fearful, that says, "You know what? We shouldn't have tried this. I'm not taking any more risks. Let's go. Let's get out of here." We also have a mystical voice of Spirit that says, "My God, we're cradled by something incomprehensible." And paradoxically, we have a blind one who feels most comfortable in the unknown, who says, "I'm not going back to anything false, because this touchstone I've chanced upon is as I've always known. There is no going back."

Our job is to be the conductor of these voices, so we can discern our true inheritance. We could say this is the proper role of will. And as we wander authentically through the days, as we meet beautiful things and harsh things, as we meet obstacles and stumble unexpectedly into joy, we're asked which side of us will meet the day: the voice in us that believes in nothing, or the one that believes in everything, or the one that is always afraid, or the one that when blind to the surface can see the depth? How will we make sense of what comes our way? How will we carry our one essential self?

I hear these voices every day. I just heard them yesterday at a Labor Day party that was full of life. While children were running about and adults were playing croquet, I realized it was a year ago to the day that my father died. My heart was both heavy and light all afternoon. Strange how he's been with me so much since he's gone. How did he carry his one essential self?

We never talked about such things. But this morning, I'm sitting in the garage holding his tools, turning his worn chisel in my hand, and wondering what I'm bringing forward from him.

It seems our conversation with life never stops, even with those who are gone. It seems the challenge of inner maturity is not to play seesaw with the joy and sorrow we face, but to open our heart like a worn basin near the edge of the sea, letting joy and sorrow swirl into a presence that lifts us in a way we never imagined.

To bring forward what genuinely speaks to us, rather than what rises out of reflex or obligation. This is being faithful to our true inheritance.

QUESTIONS TO WALK WITH

- We each have within us: a voice of fear, a voice that is certain that life rests on nothing, as well as a voice that believes in the mystery of everything, and a humble one who sees through our blindness. Without censoring yourself, begin an earnest conversation in your journal with one of these very personal voices that you carry, and let the others join in. Just see where it goes and what you learn from this.

• In conversation with a friend or loved one, describe a time when you had to wait in order to know what was true for you, in order to know what you needed to do next. Describe what this waiting felt like and what you learned from having to be patient.

19

Our Original Talent

Dive into the ocean hidden in your chest,
and discover a new world in yourself.

—Attar

In July 2012, my wife, Susan, and I drove to Auburn Hills, north of Detroit, to meet the legendary rock star Steven Tyler. Steven has been a longtime reader of my spiritual daybook *The Book of Awakening.* As his guests, we had the afternoon together before experiencing an iconic Aerosmith concert.

In meeting Steven, it was apparent that he has a large and tender heart. He's one of those seekers who is completely who he is, living very close to life. I believe this is the beginning of all talent: a commitment to lean the soul into the world. It was a gift to feel the person Steven is and later to see him inhabit his voice. The band is a tribe of master musicians, and their seamless inhabiting of eighteen classic songs in two hours mesmerized and enlivened a sold-out crowd of twenty-four thousand people.

We were standing behind the sound crew on the side of the stage and had a unique view of Steven, the band, and the short-term community that came alive throughout the evening. And watching Steven give his all was a lesson in authenticity.

No matter where he moved, thousands leaned in Steven's direction, and I thought, *If we could only understand the gift of this energy.* All of us were on our feet, swaying with our arms in the air. I looked out into the sea of arms and voices and, for this long moment, we were one organism, one wave of humanity. We were together though we didn't know each other. We didn't know who we are, what we do, where we come from, what we believe, what we like or dislike, how we've been hurt, or how we've been healed. We didn't know if we were Democrats or Republicans, Christians, Jews, or Muslims. We didn't know if we were innocent or jaded. Yet in this cavernous public space, we were all briefly lit by the truth of the music and the authenticity of this one being, giving his all. This is the power of holding nothing back.

Beneath the enormous talent of the band, beneath the singular voice coming out of Steven, it was clear that when anyone dares to be completely who they are, that thoroughness stirs our possibility out of its sleep. I think this is why we save our money, drive vast distances, and gather the way we do—to meet our own possibility. We may think it's for the music or the gifted guitar player or the once-in-a-generation actor or the poet of our time, but I believe when one flower fully blooms, the others—not yet open—begin to open. I'm starting to see that there are infinite gifts scattered among us, so we can do this for each other, over and over again. Being so fully present releases the unconscious influence we have on one another, which touches us beneath all our troubles and differences.

When opened this way, when tasting our own authenticity, we're kinder and more able to listen, more able to receive each other, and the bond between living things is strengthened. How to make these qualities and bonds last—especially in the face of difficulty—is the challenge that every generation faces, that we face now.

Of course, being human, we often fear our own possibility and try to cover it or muffle it with drugs or alcohol or sex or money or the noise of worry. But the aliveness we're born with can't be suppressed. Whenever we encounter *unmitigated aliveness*—in a flower, a bird, a river, or a person—we're awakened to where it lives in us. For the unfiltered light and pulse of being—through which we're brought alive, kept alive, and made tender—is our original talent. While there are skills to learn in order to express, the effort that sustains us is the animation of heart that lets us know our aliveness directly.

Song in particular has a strong and sacred lineage as a conduit for our aliveness. Blues and gospel music are potent examples of how song can liberate us from the weight of daily living and the oppression of others. Bernice Johnson Reagon, founder of the all-woman, African American a cappella group Sweet Honey in the Rock, speaks to the power and comfort of hymns and ballads during the civil rights movement. She bears witness to how the oldest songs were personalized to the times. By singing together during protests and marches, massive crowds could speak their particular truth and sustain their integrity.

The name Sweet Honey in the Rock comes from Psalm 81,

which alludes to a land so fertile that when rocks in that soil are cracked, honey drips from them. This is a perfect metaphor for the sweetness that waits to be released between us, if we can endure the cracks. This is the reward for daring to meet our possibility. This is the result of caring for each other in the open.

Resilience has always had to do with helping each other up and with turning something necessary into something beautiful. Like so many others, I long for resilience. As a Jew from an immigrant family decimated by the Holocaust, as a cancer survivor, and as a poet seeking to reveal what can last, I'm compelled to squeeze the lone drop of honey from the stone.

Resilience, it seems, has to do with the improbable belief that there *is* honey in the stone, and that sweet things extracted from hard things will heal us. In this, resilience might be a human element, like light or water, without which we wither. If this is true, then we would do well to study this mysterious resource which, when all else fails, somehow lands us back in our lives.

The concert ended that night with Steven singing his classic song "Dream On," which he wrote and cast out ahead of his life when he was seventeen. That night, he was lifted from under the stage and came into view playing a white piano. His voice seemed to rise from his stomach, up through his heart, and out his mouth, "Dream on, Dream on, Dream on. . . ."

Regardless of the shape the dream takes, no matter how different it might unfold from when we dreamt it, we're asked to put down our judgments, our fears, and our worries till we sway together through the burdens of our time. We're asked to stay authentic and to keep dreaming till our heart comes alive—to stay possible and awake till your aliveness sparks mine. Dream on till the honey that sleeps in the rock of our stubbornness makes its sweetness known.

This is the beginning of all talent: a commitment to lean the soul into the world.

QUESTIONS TO WALK WITH

- In your journal, describe an artist, musician, actor, or writer you admire and the aliveness they carry and express. Describe one aspect of your own possibility that you see modeled in their aliveness.

- In conversation with a friend or loved one, discuss a concert, play, public reading, art exhibit, or movie that brought you more alive. Discuss what happened during this experience and how it impacted you.

20

INITIATING THE GIFT

I OFTEN EXPERIENCE the days like someone rowing, and each time I slip an oar below the surface, it disturbs the water. When I'm tired or stunned enough to stop rowing, the water goes clear. In those moments, I can see through to the bottom. It always makes me wonder where I'm going. This is how we live. We need to move through the world, but only when we stop does the world open.

We see differently when rowing than when letting the water go clear. There seems to be a second sight waiting below our surface sight. Oh, we can see enough to get around, cross the street, go to the bank, and pick up the medicines we need. But each of us sees more clearly when the water of all that needs to be done goes clear. When still enough, a larger, more encompassing perspective opens and we see and feel more than the weather of circumstance we're moving through.

When time opens, we can see briefly from all perspectives at once and from the longest view of time. In such moments, the course of many lives is glimpsed, which we sometimes struggle to make sense of. We're stunned in such moments and utter phrases like "When exhausted, I saw my destiny," or "In the midst of my pain, I felt the pain of the world," or "When planting the last row of corn, I felt the hand of everyone who ever planted."

This deeper seeing waits in the center of our heart for us to exhaust the world's instructions, waiting for the day when we're broken open. Then, over time or all at once, the light, making its way into our break, causes us to stretch and grow, which can feel like a deep, alarming pain, one we try to quiet or get rid of. When blessed, that stretch of growth doesn't go away, and our deeper self begins to show itself, a sensation we don't often know what to do with.

Then we wake on rainy days thinking, *If I could take my dream of the future and open it in this moment, as if there's no other time to live it but now, I might initiate my gift.*

We might feel this initiation as the urge to paint, though we don't know how to paint; or the urge to stand on a certain rock by a certain sea, though we've never been to that coast; or the urge to ask our oldest friend if she is afraid to die, though we've never talked about death. The appearance of such an urge is our deeper being looking for a way into the world. If we should follow this quiet urge to live, our gift will begin to fill us the way a hand fills a glove.

Feeling this urge to see and live more deeply is another way to describe grace, when our being is close to our doing, and anything we do with our gift in that moment—helping an old woman who fainted to a shady seat, or taking a turtle from the hot pavement and putting it back in the grass, or bringing a friend who dreams of carving wood to a field of fallen cherry trees—anything we do in that moment will bring us closer to the depth of life.

For much of our lives, we carry our gifts around in a small emergency kit that rattles open when we're hurt or shaken. But there's another way to understand emergency—as any instance that allows for the agency of our emergence to take place. In this regard, life draws us out, until our deeper ways of being become how we live—feeling, when we can, our connection to all life and all time.

If we could take our dreams of the future and open them in this moment, as if there's no other time to live them but now, we might initiate our gift.

Questions to Walk With

- Meditation is an attempt to stop rowing and let the water of life go clear, so you can see through to the bottom of things. Let's try this now. Put down your oars and drift. Center yourself and breathe slowly. Whatever the day holds can wait. The first oar to leave alone is your mind. Inhale and exhale deeply. The second oar to ungrip is the oar of fear and worry. Inhale and exhale slowly. Simply breathe and let the water of your life settle and calm. Let your breathing quiet the ripples. Let the water of all life settle and calm. Look through the calm, not searching for anything, just seeing what's there.

- In conversation with a friend or loved one, describe a dream you have for your future and what it would look like if you were to live that dream now.

21

THE ART OF BEING SENSITIVE

The artist's struggle for . . . integrity must be
considered as a . . . metaphor for the struggle, which
is universal and daily, of all human beings on the face
of this globe to get to become human beings.
—JAMES BALDWIN

GIVEN THE STORMS that life brings, much of our work is to
open our heart and lean into whatever we meet. But once open,
we're not very practiced at what to do with all the feelings and
experiences that open living brings. Once sensitized to life,
how do we receive and deal with the endless cascade of feelings
that move through us?

To embody our sensitivity, we need to sustain a balance between what comes into us and what comes out of us, just as
when we breathe. Often, we spend so much time keeping things
in that we seldom realize that our fullness and strength of being
is released when we complete the cycle by letting things out.
When inner and outer complete each other, the incandescence

of life glows. Our job as spirits in bodies is to let our individual spirit rise from within to meet and inhabit the world, every chance we get. For the art of being sensitive is not sentimental but diligent and demanding, as sweet and rigorous as a Chopin nocturne.

The art of being sensitive strengthens our resilience when we dare to love what is. Loving what is means accepting the truth of whatever moment we are in. But loving what is also means keeping our heart open long enough to feel and accept everything else that is happening at the same time—around us and beyond us. By feeling our way through what we're given, we enter a heartfelt ring of awareness that keeps expanding. We feel the pain we're carrying, and then the light on the oak we're sitting near, and then the laugh of a child playing across the street, and then the wind lifting the hawk gliding above us, and how the sun casts its warmth on so many lives moving through their own pain and joy in the same exact moment.

The reward for being sensitive is that we're held by the Universe, the way the ocean in its buoyancy holds up a raft. To love what's beyond our own particular instant of living, we're asked not to minimize what we're going through or to distract ourselves from the truth of what we're going through. More deeply, we're asked to *inform* what we're going through with the vibrancy of all other life living at the same time.

The same dynamic holds for how we love each other. If while truly listening to you, I'm drawn to the sunlight behind you and hear birdsong above you, then this is more than being distracted. If loving you leads me to the sunlight and birdsong, perhaps I'm meant to bring these resources to you in your pain, just when you can't access them. This is one of the gifts of being sensitive and loving each other. In an immediate way, I'm called to give my full attention to you in your distress. And in a simultaneous, eternal way, I'm called to give my attention to everything around you that is not in distress. So I can be a conduit, bringing the restorative energies of life through me to you in your pain. To be sensitive is to be a thorough conduit.

Ultimately, the art of being sensitive supports our efforts to be who we are everywhere. And as warmth softens and opens the earth, another reward for being sensitive is that we are brought to the surface and made tender. Still, everyone struggles with the urge to stay hidden. In truth, the most hidden individuals in the world today are the closet authentics. The irony is that we share a great kinship in this struggle to be real, though we all think we're alone.

In the modern world, we tend to live an either-or existence with our sensitivity, thinking we must reveal ourselves completely or not at all. We're intimate with our small, private tribe while staying hidden in public. The great Danish philosopher Kierkegaard said, "We're all spies for God." I think he means that we all experience the depth and mystery of life but guard our deepest sensibilities and keep them secret. And so we live like spiritual spies.

Painfully, we don't know how to be sensitive and authentic in public. We don't know how to expand our tribe of intimates. We don't know how to be in conversations about what's true. A great challenge of our age is to develop the skills to offer respectful invitations to deeper conversations and more authentic relationships. Some people will reject our invitation, which is fine, and some will say, "Thanks, let me think about this." And some will drop their shoulders and utter, "My God, I thought I was alone."

Just how do we inhabit the vast, sweet terrain between being completely hidden and completely known? How do we have conversations that matter? No one knows how to do this. But this is our work in finding each other. This is our work in knitting the fabric of life back together wherever it is torn.

To be sensitive is to be a thorough conduit.

QUESTIONS TO WALK WITH

- In your journal, describe your history of being sensitive. Has it always been a struggle for you to be sensitive? Have you had to struggle with being too sensitive? Name one reward you've experienced for being sensitive and name one challenge you've experienced for being sensitive.

- In conversation with a friend or loved one, describe a time you struggled with the extremes of a strong feeling. Did you shut down to this feeling or find yourself drowning in it? Where did you finally land? What has this experience taught you?

22

CHASING PARADISE

The only protection I can offer [my son] is allowing
him to see everything with his own eyes so he can
confront just how vulnerable life is.

—EMAD BURNAT, A PALESTINIAN PHOTOGRAPHER

IT'S TAKEN YEARS, but I'm beginning to understand that chasing Paradise keeps us from living here in paradise. It's the journey and process that matter, not where we're going or where we think we're going.

Initially, we're pulled into life, drawn into a thoroughness that brings us alive. But once in the thick of it, we get tangled in the details and start to map and manage life instead of living it. When encumbered this way, life seems to be other than where we are. Or so we think. Until some shock of love or suffering jars us into a state of thoroughness that brings us back alive.

Sometimes we think we can study our way out of our entanglements. But though we can map a frog's innards, we can't know the life of a frog by pinning it to a board—any more than we can know the life of a person by naming their psychology, or the life of a community by naming its ideology. Because nothing stands still, not us or the Universe we wake in. Everything is shifting—breaking through, growing, blossoming, shedding, turning to mulch, and breaking ground again. We can only know life by living it.

In her novel *The Lake and the Lost Girl*, Jacquelyn Vincenta says, "[People] will get angry if you try to take their stories away . . . because those stories are their personal maps of the world."

And yet we're constantly challenged to drop below our own story in order to understand and feel the Whole of Life that is always beyond our own particular map. Otherwise, we make everything conform to our biased view of life. Otherwise, we superimpose the silhouette of our wounds and slights on everyone we meet. Otherwise, we remain trapped in our own web of assumptions and conclusions and never grow. Soon, we're prisoners of our own perception, mistaking the map for the earth it represents, mistaking our assumptions and conclusions for the unnameable reality we move through. Then we can easily dismiss anything or anyone that doesn't fit our personal map of life.

Here's a telling example. In the 1960s, American sociologists characterized the Burmese people as being overrun with "economic irrationality," because these reflective village people emphasized the spiritual over the material. The anthropologist Melford Spiro remarked at the time, "They build pagodas, support monasteries, and maintain monks, while they themselves reside in thatched huts, live on simple fare, and so on." The anthropologist George Foster added, "They spend lavishly on religious displays, and manifest little interest in saving (much less investing) . . . they are, it is often said, 'improvident.'"

I'm reminded of the anonymous graffiti found in a bathroom in Georgia that reads, "Those who don't hear the music think the dancers mad." Improvident and irrational according to who?

Clearly, a deeper providence and reasoning guides the Burmese people to care for the invisible threads that keep all of life connected, a providence and reasoning inaudible to those obsessed with the accumulation of wealth. This raises a fundamental difference between the mind of self-interest and the heart of impeachable connection. The mind of self-interest is fueled by the concept of ownership, while the heart of connection renews itself by participating in the circulation of life-force between all living things. While the mind of self-interest is forever engaged in the push-pull of have and have not, the heart of connection is forever engaged in the give-and-take of what keeps us all alive. The self-referential map of these anthropologists, no matter how well educated, precluded their inquiry into a story different from their own.

Humbly, when chasing wealth, we're distracted from discovering the richness inherent in our lives. When chasing love, we're distracted from the love we trip over en route to what we think is a greater love. And when chasing fame and celebrity, we're distracted from the nest of our own worth and miss the things around us to celebrate.

Beneath our inevitable entanglements in the details of life, beneath our want to study our way out of these entanglements, beneath our dependence on our personal maps of the world, each of us carries a portion of the Universal Spirit that lives in all of us. Just as the air that resides in our lungs is very personal, though it's comprised of the common air that makes up the atmosphere, the portion of Spirit that is ours to carry in this incarnation is very personal, though the Spirit our soul is made of is Universal.

As we breathe, we take in air until it fills our lungs. Once inside us, it's impossible to discern what part of that air is yours or mine and what part came from the sky. Likewise, as our heart breathes, we take in Spirit from the Universe until it fills our individual soul. Once inside us, it's impossible to discern what part of the vastness of Spirit is yours or mine and what part came from the timeless reservoir of Spirit. As healthy lungs keep us alive by exchanging the air that flows in and out of us, a healthy heart keeps us vital by exchanging the Spirit that flows in and out of us.

Earlier, I mentioned the traditional Hindu greeting *namaste*, which means "I honor the piece of the Universe that resides in you." Implicit in this greeting, always offered with a bow, is the acknowledgment that, unique and individual as we are, we carry the same timeless Spirit within us. And so our personal stories mix with the One Story we're all a part of, whether we acknowledge this or not.

When we can live our stories and not be ruled by them, we love ourselves into being. There is a Spanish saying, *Se tu vida,* which means "Be your life." This is all that is asked of us. And yet, in doing so, we can get lost in all that living engenders.

No one can determine what it means for you to be your life. We simply need to be who we are everywhere. Every time we manage to do this, it adds to our strength and view of the Whole and empowers others to be who they are everywhere. In this way, we water the seeds of decency, always in our care.

We're constantly challenged to drop below our own story in order to understand and feel the Whole of Life that is always beyond our own particular map.

QUESTIONS TO WALK WITH

- In your journal, describe one way in which you've chased your own version of Paradise and how this chasing has kept you from living the actual gifts that are around you.

- In conversation with a friend or loved one, describe someone in your life whom you had a limited view of. How did you discover that they are more than your initial perception of them? When you can, tell this person how your understanding of them has grown.

23

As We Keep Searching

Last night, the moon was twice its size, though it
never changes. Today, my heart is twice its size,
though it never rests. From this, I know I am
everything and nothing.

—MN

At first, I passed you by, as I have passed the sap oozing from
the maple, as I have passed the truth seeping from the quiet ones.
Now I hear birds wing out of view like spirits long gone from the
Earth. Now, when strangers ask, I hesitate, not holding back,
just unsure how to climb into each other's lives without breaking
anything. I keep searching through the things of this world for
one to carve into some form of hope, the kind that knits the
living together. The truth is that in losing my way, I have found
the small fire that can never go out, though we are terrified it will.

Still, there is an insidious web of influence that keeps us
from being completely where we are. This web begins at an early
age, when we're mis-educated to think that we live before a

constant audience, warned that someone is always watching and judging us. We're raised to believe that it's a terrible thing to disappoint those who are watching, even if we can't figure out what would please them. This blind fear of disappointing those who are ready to judge us somehow convinces us that life needs to be made more special than it is.

All this puts enormous pressure on us from the moment we wake to the moment we go to sleep. It hurries us toward a want for approval that is always out of reach. It took almost dying for me to realize that no one is watching. This doesn't mean we live alone or in a vacuum, but that it's more important what others feel than what others think. It means that we're not scampering in some emotional labyrinth chasing praise like some piece of cheese we can't quite see.

In truth, when we can shed all the expectations and judgments we weave, feeling the bareness of things is magical enough. With nothing in the way, the smooth feel of stone and the mist of blue that coats the night are more than enough. Without any covering, the Whole of Existence leads to itself. And we're surprised to arrive without having gone anywhere.

Given our entanglements, one of the most difficult acts of presence is not to vanish when overwhelmed by conflict or hardship. The simplest teachers in nature, such as the sun, the birds, and the flowers, are quietly heroic in this regard, not because they achieve anything, but because they remain completely true to their own nature, regardless of what happens to them.

Consider the constancy of the sun. Even in the womb, before our eyes are formed, we can feel the warmth and light of the sun through our mother's belly. Spirit works this way, warming us before we can see, walk, or talk. As we grow, the heart senses the undying warmth of Spirit regardless of how blind we are to what we struggle with. Our job is to trust what the heart senses ahead of our understanding.

Under all our struggle, life exists independent of our assumptions or judgment. Life is not human-centric. I experienced this firsthand with my loss of hearing. The day I received my hearing aids, I walked out of the office and heard birdsong for the first time in months. I hadn't even realized I wasn't hearing birdsong. Of course, the birds never stopped their glorious melodies because I was losing my hearing. I'm not sure what kind of bird was singing that day, but hearing it again made me cry. That moment extinguished the self-centered philosophical question "If a tree falls in the forest and no one is there to hear it, does it make a sound?" Of course it does!

And like the birds that sing at the first sight of light, our hearts don't stop loving because we in our pain are blind, deaf, or afraid. Though from the depths of our fear and pain, we can muffle the love that emanates from our heart. We can convince ourselves that we're no longer loving. In our hurt and confusion, we can deny the love that keeps shining from within us.

Yet we can always access the love in our hearts by finding our courage, which meant originally "to stand by one's core." Imagine a mountain rising from the earth. No matter how closely we look, it's impossible to tell where the mountain ends and the earth it rises from begins. But it's the earth that makes the mountain strong.

In the same way, you can't tell where the soul stops and where the ground of being it rises from begins. When we can stand by our core, we enter our authority of being, which gains its strength from the Universal Ground of Being that is its foundation. So when we stand by our core, we stand by the core of all things. When we enter our center, we touch into the center of all things.

Still none of this is easy, even when aware of it. And so we take guidance wherever we can, even from the forest floor, where we can ask the smallest flower, "What lets you bloom though no one is watching?"

When we can still ourselves, our heart will sink—of its own weight—below the noise of the world, the advice of others, and even our own expectations. When that still, we are by our core. This is how we practice meeting life.

So when losing track of what I believe in, when wondering what I'm called to next, I still my heart until I stop feeding the dark things that keep shouting they're important. In that stillness, I ask myself, Where is the light coming from today? What do I have to do to put myself in its path? What part of me is illuminated for leaning into life? What can I learn by being so lighted? What is it my heart can't keep from doing that will bring me more alive?

To lean into life requires a quiet courage that lets us find our aliveness. And the reward for leaning into life is that everything hidden becomes sweet and colorful. Or more, we're finally present enough to receive the sweetness and color that is always there. Consider how a flower opens. It doesn't prepare for a particular moment but stays true to a life of opening and leaning toward the light. When a flower blossoms, it turns inside out and wears its beauty in the world. In just this way, a soul opens over a lifetime of leaning into life.

Despite the hardships we encounter, and in spite of our pain, the heart keeps opening after closing, the way day follows night—until meeting life is our daily experiment in truth. No matter the obstacles, we're asked to welcome all the teachers we encounter along the way, each shouting and whispering that the secret kingdom is everywhere.

As we keep searching, these efforts never go away: the work of presence, the listening for teachers, and the vow to stay close to the fire of our aliveness. I confess, when I began, I wanted to light so many things. Now I'm the one being lighted and there's nowhere to go. I can see that as being becomes a nest, there's no reason to fly.

When we can shed all the expectations
and judgments we weave, feeling the bareness
of things is magical enough.

QUESTIONS TO WALK WITH

- In your journal, describe the web of influence you are under and trace where these expectations and judgments come from. Identify one expectation or judgment that feels inaccurate and how you might put it down.

- In conversation with a friend or loved one, describe a moment when you stood by your core. When standing by your core, did you feel or sense the core of all things? What did this feel like? What led you to this moment? What steps can you take to stand by your core when you need to?

24

OUR DREAM OF LIFE

IMAGINE A YOUNG woman living on top of a large, majestic mountain. Imagine that she walks through the pristine streams and sits before the vast vistas every day. Imagine that she's lonely and in search of what is real, with no sense of how majestic the ground is where she walks. This is how we go through life sometimes, searching for what is under our feet.

Now imagine on a breezy summer day that this lonely young woman—dreaming of a life that matters while living a life that matters—sees a goldfinch up close. She's never seen anything quite so delicate and beautiful. And the beautiful, delicate bird won't land but flits its colorful wings as if it were sent to tease her. Secretly, she wants to fly like the goldfinch. Perhaps the finch would bestow its lightness on her and quiet her loneliness, if only she could touch it.

Yearning for the goldfinch occupies her summer, which comes and goes, as does the fall. Life on the mountain enters winter, and she hasn't seen the goldfinch in months. But the bright yellow bird is now the symbol of what she yearns for. So she chases this image in her mind, in her sleep, in her conversations with strangers. All the while, the very real and majestic ground she stands on keeps emanating its beauty.

The following summer she anticipates the bright yellow bird, as if her life depends on it. At last, the little yellow bird appears, and its beauty slows her mind until she simply watches rather than chases. Mysteriously, this is when the small beautiful bird lands on the back of her hand. In that moment, our lonely seeker is no longer lonely, for her dream of life and her very life have finally kissed.

What she does next will liberate or burden her. If she sees the bird landing on her hand as a fleeting moment of fulfillment, she will be trapped, chasing her dream of life while ignoring her actual life. But if, in this lighted moment, she can accept that the finch in its beauty carried her dream of life until she was ready to accept the beauty in her own life, then she will thank the bird as it flies off, knowing that what matters has always been waiting in the ground she walks.

The journey to inner freedom includes this process of loving something outside of us until it can awaken an aspect of our own soul. For the woman, it was a goldfinch. For my father, it was his love of sailing. For some, it's a love of turtles or a love of painting. For me it's a love of questions, because I long to open my heart, and a love of poetry, because I long to discover how everything is connected. The crucial turning point in our journey from effort to grace is whether we finally accept that the thing we chase and love waits to be awakened within us. No matter what we dream of, what we long for holds an instruction for how we can find what matters in the life we're already living.

The journey to inner freedom includes this process of loving something outside of us until it can awaken an aspect of our own soul.

QUESTIONS TO WALK WITH

- Meditate on a dream you've been chasing or working toward, something you long for. Close your eyes and breathe slowly. Try to visualize the dream hovering before you, complete. Inhale deeply and take in the image of your completed dream. Hold your dream before you and imagine it's a mirror of your soul waiting to come alive. Open your eyes and try to see your dream as an image of what lives within you.

- In your journal, translate what you're longing for into something that already lives within you, and describe what steps you need to take to enliven the dream you carry within.

25

STANDING ON AND STANDING FOR

Give me a place to stand on and I will move the Earth.
—ARCHIMEDES

THERE ARE TWO perennial questions we need to ask in order to find each other and our way in the world. They are: *What am I standing on?* and *What am I standing for?*

Standing on refers us back to a timeless foundation, to some sense of Source, to all that is larger than us from which we're renewed as integral beings. *Standing for* leads us into the heart of what we value and the ethics by which we live in the world. *Standing on* gives us a compass. *Standing for* gives us a direction to stay true to by following that compass. The two perennial questions need to be asked of ourselves and everyone we meet. They are a basis for honest relationship.

What we stand on is inextricably linked to what we stand for. Consider how a simple lever works. Using a pivot point known as a fulcrum, one weight can leverage the lift of another weight. With our commitment as the fulcrum, what we stand on gives us leverage to empower what we stand for. In this way, who we are leverages what we do in the world. But without knowing what we stand on, what we stand for can become hollow. Without knowing our foundation, we can become overbearing in our opinions.

There are always two sides of knowing. One is the quest for meaning, the endless forging of what is essential in order to live. The other is our attachment to a particular view, idea, feeling, or belief. This is the trap of conviction: the stubbornness that turns truth into an assumption or conclusion. It's the trap of conviction that has Israelis and Palestinians distrust each other without ever having met, while young Christians in the Midwest run with no reason from Islamic children.

As Jon Kabat-Zinn puts it, "If you're too convicted in your opinions or beliefs, perhaps you are a convict, imprisoned within the confines of your own understandings." In this way, unquestioned convictions are old thoughts hardened into seldom-tested beliefs. Instead of bringing us closer to life and each other, our hardened views enforce patterns that keep us from reclaiming the common ground we all stand on.

Part of the riddle of being human resides in this question: If love and truth are in us, why are they so hard to find and grow between us? It seems that love and truth wait like seeds within us. If never watered, they never grow.

But if what lives in us is watered, the vastness of life enters our heart like rain soaking seeds waiting in soil. In time, there's a fertile silence that takes the place of words as we break surface, and living with that, our pains give way to joy.

How vastness enters our heart is part of the human journey. For everyone will be dropped into the depth of life. What matters is how we meet that moment and who comes with us. Meeting that chance is how the deeper journey of life begins. For me, that chance was my journey through cancer. It changed my stance in the world. It made me a student of all paths and all traditions. It made me a student of applied Spirit. It led me to what I stand on and stand for.

But it doesn't have to be illness or catastrophe that grounds us. It can be wonder, beauty, love, or surprise. Great love and great suffering come to us all, to remind us how rare it is to be here at all. Then it's our job to stay awake and aware, kind and loving. Ultimately, we're challenged to find something lasting to stand on and something noble to stand for.

Being human is such a mystery, filled with blessings and hardships, often one leading to the other. And through my own spin from blessing to hardship and back, I've learned that when all else fails, I'm often forced to stand exactly where I am until the ground of being that lives forever comes up through my feet, making me a little more solid.

So I invite you to reflect on what you stand on. What is your deepest bedrock, your foundation? How does it solidify your place in this life? And what do you stand for? What are the values and ethics that guide your truest actions in the world? In a personal way, how is what you stand on related to what you stand for?

I invite you to reflect on your hardened convictions, obsessions, and excesses, as a way to diagnose what keeps you from what you stand on. I invite you to listen to your experience, as a way to put down what's in the way. For inner work begins with the vow to get closer to life.

Standing on and standing for are endless quests for how

we in our fullness can keep the world together. I only know that when a flower finally opens, it accepts everything that comes from the sky. And when a heart finally opens, it accepts everything about existence. And when loving wholeheartedly, we can make honey out of anything. The river of who we are runs through every country. It ignores all borders. Our call is to follow that river.

Ultimately, we're challenged to find something lasting to stand on and something noble to stand for.

QUESTIONS TO WALK WITH

- In your journal, describe one way you are trapped in your own convictions, one way you are too stubborn about something you believe in. How can you update and refresh this conviction or belief?

- In conversation with a friend or loved one, take turns describing what each of you stands on and what you stand for. Then discuss one aspect of your personal history that you both have in common.

26

Slowly Is the Way

The Artist is no other than he who unlearns what he
has learned, in order to know himself.

—E. E. Cummings

Today, you actually have to defend your time in order
to have a long thought.

—James Taylor

When a dear friend was hiking up Mount Kilimanjaro, the
temptation was to walk at a brisk pace to make headway on the
day's climb. But her native guide nudged her and the others out
of their pace, saying in Swahili, *"Pole, pole n'd'muendo,"* which
means, "Slowly, slowly is the way."

We often rush to cultivate our gifts in an effort to accomplish or secure what we want or dream of, but our beauty is
released when we slow down to meet the world through what
we're given. Life will unwind us until we accept that the journey

of a soul on Earth is to discover what matters by making good use of our heart.

There are many ways to slow down, knowing that life will speed us up, many ways to quiet the race within us and around us, knowing that we will join the race again. Some of the ways we can slow down include: letting what we keep in out, facing what we avoid, putting things down, not going back to sleep once awake, and practicing the art of acceptance and deep listening.

Holding things tightly inevitably speeds us up. We can't see the beauty or power of our feelings as long as we hold them inside. This is why fear or sadness can pound excessively in our chest the longer we hide it. But once we admit that we're afraid or confess to being deeply sad, we're somewhat lightened of the burden and somehow stronger for letting the truth of where we are express itself. No matter how we resist, we're meant to let what is in out. By this vow of expression, our heaviness can start to have spaces in it. When releasing the things that build up, difficulties begin to unfold. This movement from keeping things in to letting things out is at the heart of all transformation.

We're constantly drawn into the world and yet we fear the world. In spite of our fear, what matters waits under all the ways we run and avoid. I know this because of the many times I've run from truth and the many ways I've tried to avoid what life has given me, all of which only exhausted me into landing where I am. For whenever I can face what I avoid, life reveals itself. Facing what I avoid always stills me enough to feel the very pulse of life lining every path and tree and leaf.

Another way to slow our journey is by putting down things

we cling to. For the strains of attachment pull us away from the pace of what is real. By putting down our certainty, we begin to learn from others. By putting down our desperate want for fame and greatness, we begin to experience our common journey, and this lessens our loneliness. By putting down our want to be unique, we often discover our true inheritance, which is our felt kinship with all life.

Yet even when putting things down, it is impossible to prevent heartache. No one likes heartache or loss, but they are great inevitable teachers we meet when we dare to care and love. From my own heartache, I've discovered that loss opens us to the logic of Spirit. For grief forces me to look for those I've lost everywhere, and this in turn forces me to fall in love with the world again. There's no replacing who or what has been lost. But somehow, our tears water the break in our heart so we can grow. None of this happens until we slow down, until we put down what we cling to, until we're ready to receive, unsure of what.

Another great leveler of urgency and speed is the practice of acceptance. For resistance to the truth always speeds us up. Resistance to the truth always causes suffering. Too often, we waste time—even years—in an argument with life, rather than working with life to navigate our hardships. And the great doorway to acceptance is deep listening. Not just hearing other people, but hearing ourselves. Many of us are at a loss to speak our truth, because we've stopped listening to our soul.

Practicing these ways of slowing down will help you learn how to truly speak. As fish in their grace demonstrate, it's not surfacing or bottoming that is our home, but our movement back and forth. That immersion brings us alive. For the slow work of being leads us to a thorough life, where the deeper currents moving through us are life-giving and empowering. And the Whole of Life rinsing through our heart and mind is what we feel and think and speak.

So no matter who I might be with, I try not to insist on my own language, but to slow my mind until I can hear what is common in all language. It's there I find resilience. And the feel of resilience brings me back to the crucible of my cancer journey years ago. We were all strangers, each on our own trajectory of dream, each in our own vocation, each in or out of relationship, each understanding the world in a different way. Then cancer threw us together with such speed and force, stripping us violently of all the external descriptors that we carried. Once stunned and naked, all that mattered was making it through the pain and fear together. All that mattered was helping each other make it to tomorrow.

While hardship announces itself like a storm, surviving calls for the slow balance of a tai chi master, meeting only what is necessary with a full and humble heart. It's a truth affirmed by all the saints, that when we let our heart slowly meet the world, the world reveals itself as not rapid or hidden, but simply waiting like a lake that will, from time to time, go clear.

In essence, great love and great suffering force us to be awake. Then we're asked to sustain our effort in not going back to sleep, in not going numb, in not drifting from the precious, fragile fact of our existence. This is why we need each other, to help us not go back to sleep. But how? By stopping the race, by entering the truth of any moment, by listening to the greater wisdom of life as it moves through us the way a cloud moves through the sky.

*In essence, great love and great suffering force
us to be awake. Then we're asked to sustain our
effort in not going back to sleep.*

QUESTIONS TO WALK WITH

- In your journal, describe one way that you speed up your life and how this affects you. Then describe one way you can practice slowing down and how this affects you.

- In conversation with a friend or loved one, choose one of these ways of slowing down—letting what we keep in out, facing what we avoid, putting things down, not going back to sleep once awake, or practicing the art of acceptance and deep listening—and tell the story of someone you admire and how that person practices this way of slowing down.

WIDENING OUR CIRCLE

I have walked through many lives,
some of them my own,
and I am not who I was,
though some principle of being
abides, from which I struggle
not to stray.

—STANLEY KUNITZ

With deep insight, Albert Einstein talked about the fact of our Oneness and the illusion of our separateness:

A human being is a part of the whole, called by us "Universe," a part limited in time and space. [We] experience [ourselves, our] thoughts and feelings as something separated from the rest—a kind of optical delusion of [our] consciousness. This delusion is a kind of prison for us, restricting us to our personal desires and to affection for a few persons nearest to us. Our task must be to free ourselves from this prison by widening our circle of compassion to embrace all living creatures and the whole of nature in its beauty. Nobody is able to achieve this completely but the striving for such achievement is, in itself, a part of [our] liberation and a foundation for inner security.

The great physicist encourages us to widen our circle of care as a practice that deepens our relationship to all that matters. That relationship gives us a sense of inner foundation.

He suggests that widening our circle of compassion is an act of recovering what is foundational and essential. In an everyday way, this is the work of being fully here. When stalled and bruised, we can re-engage this work by restoring trust in our firsthand experience, by reaffirming that the soul wants to join with the world, and by accepting the inner fact that we are more than what is done to us. When we can enter the widening circle in which all things are connected, the personal self is restored as a threshold to the Universe.

The chapters in this section delve into the many ways we're asked to widen our circle and how that deepens and strengthens our connections.

27

What the Elks Were Staring At

After driving for three days, a young and restless archaeologist was late for a conference in Laramie, Wyoming. Pressed and pressing, he was speeding through a sunlit basin somewhere between the vast plains and the front ridge of the Rocky Mountains when he suddenly found himself in the midst of a herd of elk. Exasperated, he honked at the herd to let him pass. They simply crowded in closer and stared at him. Forced to stop, he turned his truck off, and the herd kept him there for a long time. Then he realized they weren't staring at him, but off into the big sunlit sky behind him. When the sun began to set behind the highest ridge, they left. He sat there till the last elk was out of view. As he restarted his truck, everything seemed different. This brief encounter with a herd of elk did something to his eyes. He was no longer heading anywhere but sweetly lost in the Oneness the elk silence had opened. Now he was entering time and no longer chasing it.

This story represents yet another choice between our student-self and teacher-soul. The choice can be framed this way. From which sense of center will we live our days: as an arrow always seeking its mark, or as a drop of water always seeking its home? Half the time, we're so eager to get somewhere only because we're uncomfortable with where we are. Much of the time, we're trying so hard to keep the difficult things out that we stop letting in what is always present and beautiful.

The journey is always different than we expect and much longer than we imagine. Ultimately, life is not something to chase or push through but to enter and absorb. While this seems simple, it is one of the hardest truths to keep before us. And keeping the deeper truths before us is like wrestling a whale that has broken the surface—imploring it to stay with us in the world, though in order to survive, it has to dive back into the deep.

We could say that keeping things that matter in view is the aim of all knowledge. The great Jewish philosopher Abraham Heschel tells us that, in the eyes of the Jews of Eastern Europe, knowledge was not a means for achieving power, but a way to keep drinking from the Source of All Reality. In their eyes, study for the sake of acquiring something was considered a desecration. The aim of study was to partake of spiritual beauty. Why? As a means of staying resilient and whole.

In light of this, the little conversation between Ramana Maharshi and his student, that we discussed in an earlier chapter, invites us to make a sacred and personal practice of discerning these choices again and again: to listen to the problem-solver we carry or to the spirit within that lives beneath all problems, to deepen our doubt or our faith, to exert our will or our surrender, and whether to manipulate the world with our ego or to relate to the world with our larger self.

When tossed about by hesitation and confusion, which will happen, we can still ourselves and make a conscious assessment as to who is leading us: the student eager to manage things or the inner teacher offering us a way to apprehend things more deeply. When pressed by insecure turnings, which will happen, we can stop working the time-management quandaries that heighten our doubt and inflame our will, and try to receive the lift of the Oneness of Things.

When in the midst of crisis, which will happen, we can take the risk to believe that the work will go on by itself. When drowning in pain and sorrow, which will happen, we can summon the courage to stay with our feelings long enough to experience something deeper than our pain and sorrow. To be sure, the pragmatist in us will always feed on a divided world it must manage for us to survive. But given the chance, the larger self in us will find its place in the Universal Stream, where we will discover, again and again, the peace a small boat knows as it floats on the sea.

*The journey is always different than we expect
and much longer than we imagine.*

QUESTIONS TO WALK WITH

- In conversation with a friend or loved one, describe a moment of doubt and what you were most deeply doubting. Then describe a moment of faith and what you had faith in. Discuss what led you to each of these moments. Then describe the fundamental nature of life that exists regardless of your doubt or faith, as you understand it.

28

THE COVENANT OF PRACTICE

THERE'S A PARADOX about practice we must enter if we're to do more than chase our own tail. To start with, practice is necessary as a way to bring ourselves alive through the particulars of anything we want to learn. As the Tibetan Buddhist Jennifer Fox says:

> Understanding emerges and evolves through practice . . .
> [by] maintaining a ground in yourself that the teachings
> can soak into, which would remain abstract if there was
> no practice.

And yet, as the American spiritual teacher Adyashanti says:

> The role of spiritual practice is basically to exhaust the seeker.
> If the practice does what it's supposed to do, it exhausts our
> energy for seeking, and then reality has a chance to present
> itself.

So we're challenged to always practice the particular acts of living, knowing all the while that such immersion will only open us to the end of all practice, where unrehearsed living is its own reward.

In daily terms, we practice to apply what we learn in the future, the way a jazz pianist will rigorously learn scales and chords in order to someday improvise. In time, the ultimate reward for practice is that it delivers us more deeply into the river of the present. In this way, anything is worthy of our immersion, which in time will allow our practice to dissolve into the moment we're about to live.

Another central aspect of immersion is that under all our felt experiences, the things that matter can't be named. For what matters is not provable, only knowable. This is why, in many traditions, there is no word for God. In the Jewish tradition, a blank space is left in many holy texts where God is referred to, as a form of reverence to the unseeable Mystery. By its very nature, what is essential is as near and unseeable as air is to birds and water is to fish.

I'm reminded of the story of a man walking along the ocean. He sees two fish in the surf and wades out to meet them. He leans over and asks, "What's it like to live in the ocean?" Neither fish answers and the man moves on. Once out of view, one fish turns to the other to ask, "What's an ocean?" The closer we are to the heart of living, the harder it is to name what we're a part of, because we are *in* it. This inability to name what we're experiencing is a sign that we're fully immersed.

Once immersed in life, it's harder to hold on to things, because that's the nature of the deep. The further we go, the more we're asked to trust our knowing over our knowledge. At best, the mind is a net that, no matter how finely woven, will always have holes. But we don't have to worry, for the heart is a sponge, waiting below the mind to absorb whatever the mind can't grasp.

Once immersed, it's more important to have what matters move through us than for us to hold on to what matters. So don't fret when things that matter slip through. Your heart will receive them. For what slips through our thinking will only settle in the ground of our being despite our diligence or forgetfulness. The things that matter always settle as small treasures that drift below all reason, covered in time by the nameless bottom no one sees. There they are incorporated into the softness of all we have in common. This nameless grounding in the depth of things is a source of lasting strength.

And though our preparation requires good, hard work, in the end it only serves as kindling for the fire of aliveness that we're here to keep burning. It's our preparation that stokes the fire. At the end of our preparation, we're asked to obey the call to enter life and not just plan it.

The clear gift of practice is that we will lose ourselves in its experience. If we stay devoted to this kind of effort, we'll surrender the habit of our self in order to join with all that is larger than us until, as the German philosopher Friedrich Nietzsche suggests, what is necessary is beautiful. A good example is sitting in extended meditation—past the noise of our thoughts, past the aches of sitting, past the breathing of others sitting nearby—until we slip out of our normal self into a momentary Oneness with life beyond our mind.

In actuality, where practice and immersion meet is a form of prayer. So when feeling lost, pick up something broken and try to fix it, or listen to something natural and try to understand how it works, or just open your hands and welcome whatever lands near your heart.

On the deepest level, effort that involves our entire being often evaporates our will. Then we open like a flower wherever we are and the ground of life sends its life-giving water up through our heart into our mouth and arms, so we might show our care, which then attracts other life. The result of unmitigated practice is that the life-force that surfaces through us does what it does best—it lives and finds other life.

Yet how do we begin a practice of immersion? By giving our attention completely to any one particular aspect of life, no matter what it is, and giving ourselves to it thoroughly. For through a love of details, the Whole of Life appears. The poet Rainer Maria Rilke speaks of how the great sculptor Auguste Rodin so loved whatever was before him that beauty flowed to meet his hands. Until, as Rilke says, "the other, greater beauty [came] when all was ready for it, as animals come to drink when night holds sway and the forest is free of strangers."

Like a sponge that assumes its full shape once dipped in water, practice and the immersion it evokes let us expand and become our full potential. Like a blacksmith who dips his face in a lake after hours of forging tools, we know God the moment we enter the lake of life and break our image with a kiss.

Immersion will only open us to the end of all practice, where unrehearsed living is its own reward.

QUESTIONS TO WALK WITH

- In your journal, describe one thing you're practicing in your life. How is this practice making you more skillful? How is your immersion of effort making you more yourself?

29

Unwavering

This is the story of a dog named Hachikō, an Akita born on a farm near the city of Odate in Japan in 1923. The life of Hachikō conveys the wisdom of animals as expressed through their devotion. Hachikō lived with Hidesaburō Ueno, a professor of agriculture at the University of Tokyo. For a couple of years, Hachikō would meet Professor Ueno at the end of each day at the Shibuya railway station. But in May 1925, Professor Ueno suffered a cerebral hemorrhage and died while Hachikō was waiting for him. Every day at the same time for the next nine years, Hachikō would make his way to the Shibuya station and wait.

As Hachikō kept returning to the spot where he last saw the one he loved, commuters brought treats to sustain him during his wait. Hachikō became a legend and, as word of his devotion spread, teachers and parents told his story as an example of lasting love and friendship.

A year before Hachikō died, a sculpture was made of him

and placed near the spot of his long wait. On March 8, 1935, Hachikō was found dead on a street in Shibuya near the station. Today, the place where Hachikō waited is marked with bronze paw prints, and the nearby statue shines from the wear of commuters petting it.

Recently, we drove to Crown Point, Indiana, to bring home our new dog, an eighteen-month-old yellow lab. It's been more than a year since our beloved Mira died. And to our surprise, this new dog has called to us. Our grief has been deep, cracking us open. In our own way, we've been returning like Hachikō to the spot where we last saw the one we loved. We were waiting like Hachikō, but unsure for what.

Then, on a gray February day, we awoke somewhere in between loss and life. We couldn't imagine ever having another dog, and yet we couldn't imagine living the rest of our lives without one. We weren't sure if we were ready, but something under our grief said, "Go and see."

Driving to Crown Point, I was stunned by how easily we're transformed and rearranged by what we love. Softened by loss, our heart is imprinted with the shape of those we love for the rest of our days. And animals embody a secret that keeps us close to life. They remind me every day that each of us is about to happen.

We're calling this little one Zuzu, after a character in the 1946 movie *It's a Wonderful Life*. Zuzu is the youngest daughter of the main character, George Bailey. She brings a flower home from school and is upset when a few petals fall. George pretends to reattach them while slipping them into his pocket. Later that night, when close to suicide, he's shown how the world would be less if he'd never been born. Then he's given a second chance by God to reattach himself to life. He returns to his family, unsure if his reckoning of soul was just a desperate dream. But when he finds Zuzu's petals in his pocket, he's humbled to realize that all of it is true—the yearning, the turmoil, the letting go, and the grace.

Our Zuzu was a stray found on the streets of Kentucky, and her second chance is ours.

Every day . . . each of us is about to happen.

QUESTIONS TO WALK WITH

- In conversation with a friend or loved one, describe a person, place, or time that you return to out of love, like the loyal Akita Hachikō. Why do you do this? What does this personal pilgrimage bring to you and keep alive in you?

30

Honoring the Anonymous

We draw the circle of our family too small.
—Mother Teresa

THE SUN is a journal devoted to the truth of the human experience. It was started by Sy Safranksy more than forty years ago in a garage in Chapel Hill, North Carolina. The first issue was run on a photocopier in 1974. After more than five hundred issues and more than a hundred thousand readers, *The Sun* has become a community of people who keep the conversation of life going in this tested journal—a modern, grassroots form of the Talmud. Each issue features a Readers Write section, which is just as insightful and wise as the luminaries and artists who fill the rest of the pages.

Sy tells this story, which unfolded around the publication of the September 2007 issue:

As tens of thousands of copies of the issue were waiting at the printer to be mailed, someone called us on behalf of an inmate whose piece about prison gangs was featured in that month's Readers Write. We had sent him the final, edited version of his writing for review weeks earlier, but due to the slow prison mail system, he had only just received it. The call was to alert us that we'd neglected to sign his piece "Name Withheld," which he'd requested because he feared reprisal from gang leaders.

Because he was on death row in a maximum-security prison, we had no quick and easy way to contact him. We postponed the mailing and tested numerous methods of correcting each copy by hand, all with unsatisfactory results. We debated whether to let the issue go out with the mistake, but in the end we made the only ethical choice: to reprint more than seventy thousand issues, this time with the prisoner's piece correctly attributed to "Name Withheld."

This is an extraordinary moment of community. Why? Because Sy and his staff never lost sight of the person who had reached out to them with his truth. They accepted their responsibility for inviting this man to tell his truth in the open and faced their uneasiness in leaving him there by himself. They kept their focus on the life involved and the potential injury he faced for telling his truth.

Sy and his staff could have weighed the options. They could have said, "We tried. It's out of our hands." They could have equated the cost and effort to reprint seventy thousand copies with the exposure of one inmate who was on death row anyway. We do this all the time: we minimize the ethical situation we face as the effort required to meet the situation deepens.

Yet we're constantly challenged to transcend our pragmatic

inertia. A blind woman falls across the street. We wince, but it's a bit too far to help, and we're already late. So we think, "Someone nearby will help her." It's always hard to discern what work is ours, but when we trust our heart, it's all our work.

Considering the many ways we turn from each other, the effort of *The Sun* staff to put themselves in this inmate's place, to realize that his fear and further suffering were just as important as their own, is a deep form of courage.

Such anonymous heroism begins by following the smallest call to let our care out. The chain-smoker at the hotel is suddenly obsessed with feeding the baby ducks he walks by. The lawyer on the phone in his car says, "I'll call you back," as he swerves and stops to pick up a stray pup. And my wife carefully tries to free the agitated fly trapped between the screen and the window. Something in us cares, if we can just let that care guide us in the world.

We're all kindred spirits who keep meeting in the middle of our wonder and our pain. No matter where we begin, each honest account of what we go through starts to create a path to a larger, common, more eternal clearing where we're destined to meet everyone who ever lived.

And the center of all life—as felt in that common, eternal clearing—is life-giving and healing. This is why when you break your heart and I lose my dream, we can meet in that clearing and recognize each other. And though no one can live in that clearing, any more than we can live too close to the sun, it's the common light received from that clearing that keeps us well, enabling us to grow. It doesn't matter what we call that common, eternal clearing, as long as we honor it and return to it.

It's always hard to discern what work is ours,
but when we trust our heart, it's all our work.

Questions to Walk With

- In your journal, describe a time when you didn't reach out or lend a helping hand. Why? What kept you from getting involved? What were you afraid of?

- Take a walk in the city or town where you live and quietly and anonymously follow your care. If it leads you to watch children play, watch children play. If it leads you to help someone who's struggling with their groceries, help them with their groceries. Later, in conversation with a friend or loved one, tell the story of your anonymous care and what you've learned from it.

31

Looking at Things Freshly

Though we cannot think alike, may we not love alike?
May we not be of one heart, though we are not of one
opinion?

—John Wesley, 1749

Ironically, we spend so much time avoiding change, when
we're changing all the time. Even our cells are rearranging,
mine as I'm writing this, yours as you're reading this. It's like
trying not to blink when we've already blinked twice during
the thought.

This all came up recently when I was speaking to a survey-
of-religions class at a community college in the Midwest. A
likable young woman raised her hand. She described a group
she belonged to that held Thursday dinners with people of different faiths. As she spoke about meeting people different from
herself, her eyes lit up. Then she hit a wall, saying, "I love listening to others until it rubs up against my beliefs, the way I
was raised." Her eyes went cold, "I'm open, but I'm not going

to change who I am." Suddenly, she was digging in. Yet she was already changed by what she'd heard, only struggling to admit it.

This led to a conversation about how we harden our mind. This often comes from the quietly desperate effort to assure ourselves that who we are—or who we think we are—won't vanish or melt for being exposed to life. We fear that in our encounters with difference we'll lose our identities. We fear we'll succumb and become what we encounter. On the contrary, the essence of who we are will only *grow* for listening to others. Healthy change is called growth, and it reflects how we *become* who we are by encountering the various energies of life as met in others. As Thomas Merton said, If we truly beheld one another, "we would fall down and worship each other."

I remember that, for a long time, I found myself acclimating to not hearing, before admitting that I needed hearing aids, and slowly the dullness of a quiet world began to appear normal. Likewise, when we acclimate to the comfort of our own views and resist any form of difference, we become *mind-deaf*, which means that we impose our dullness of thinking on the world and consider it normal. Being mind-deaf, we think that understandings of life are only valid if they are close to our own. When we acclimate to the history of our own feelings and resist the truth of other people's feelings, we become *heart-deaf* and feel that experiences of life are only valid if they mirror our own. Some degree of this resistance happens to everyone. The question is, How long can we refuse the lessons that come from understandings and experiences other than our own?

When we resist every thought we meet unless it upholds our

own thinking, we're turning everything we see into us. And when we minimize or invalidate every feeling we meet, unless it confirms our own experience, we're turning everything we touch into us. These extensions of self-centeredness starve the mind and heart into isolation, and such acts of self-centeredness drain us and the life of those around us.

There's a thin line between adapting to what life brings our way and colluding in our own diminishment by acclimating to the comfort of habits that box us in. Often, this collusion stems from our resistance to change. Our insistence on the stories we prefer can encase us, until we're wrapped and tangled in a hardened web of self that no longer lets us drink from the well of life.

As it is, we seldom see what's up close clearly and often take the things we love for granted. Until we're stunned or pained into looking at things freshly. Not because we don't care, but because this is the foreground and background of consciousness, the approach and retreat of wakefulness. I've come to understand this seeing and not-seeing as a natural, if dangerous, ebb and flow of being here.

So how do we begin to expand our view? By revitalizing our ability to take in the Whole of Life and to act from there. Some of you may remember that before GPS devices, there were AAA TripTiks. You'd call up the American Automobile Association, tell them where you were going, and they would plot a route on a physical map, highlighted in yellow, so you could find your way. If you made a wrong turn, however, you'd have to retrace your steps to the highlighted route to resume your journey.

With GPS, you can redirect yourself from wherever your

journey takes you. You don't have to backtrack and start over. This is because the reference point for GPS is global, as seen from satellites. The AAA TripTiks, helpful as they were, assumed there was only one way to get where you were going. The GPS encourages whole-mind thinking and assumes there are many ways to get where you're going. It allows for exploration and course correction. In an age where everyone's lives are more connected than ever, we need to move through the world with an awareness that there are many ways to get where we're going.

So much depends on letting in more views than our own. The profound feminist thinker Carol Lee Flinders quotes Huston Smith about our need to have more than one perspective, no matter how strongly we believe in any one idea:

> [He] used to talk about the value of being able to see through two eyes—that if one of our eyes is covered, we don't see depth. Look out from two eyes, and you see the point of convergence way out ahead where things cohere, and then everything becomes multidimensional.

We need more than one perspective to glimpse the point of convergence where all perspectives meet. When we become zealous or stubborn, when we stay resistant to change, we're seeing with one eye and lose the common center from where all views emerge and return.

We vacillate between resisting change and accepting change, between acclimating to our own views and adjusting to the unknown. We teeter back and forth between being mind-deaf and heart-deaf and being forced to let in other views. And yet we must try to go deep without drowning, always working toward the point of convergence.

I have to confess that, after a lifetime of experience, I still wake some days feeling small. When smaller than I really am, it's hard to stay connected to everything larger than me. It's hard to lean forward. When smaller than I really am, I start to see with only one eye. And then I start to hide. I start to distrust. I settle into being disheartened, though I know better. Having endured these shifts several times in my life, I know that the storm of being small will pass. When feeling small, when feeling less than, when unable to reach out the way I know I can, it's important to remember the point of convergence where we all meet.

What a world we live in, where small things of color fly about us and sing, a world so much bigger than the frames my mind can put around it. Diversity and change underline the day, whether I acknowledge it or not. But only when I can stay open to the changes and look at things freshly, can I in time say yes again to life.

*So much depends on letting in
more views than our own.*

QUESTIONS TO WALK WITH

- In your journal, speak of a time when you resisted change even as it was happening. What did this cross-purpose do to you? How did you come to finally accept the change?

- In conversation with a friend or loved one, tell the story of a point of convergence that you arrived at with someone very different from you. How did you find common ground?

32

A CHILD OF THE SIXTIES

I AM A child of the 1960s, that wild and vital time, so misunderstood, exalted, or condemned, based on the glimpses of its extremes. It was a turbulent, wondrous time that shaped so many of us. I could list so many events, and each has a story worth telling. We were carried on a current of social upheaval that suspended and broke the roles awaiting my generation. We happened to grow up on a cultural fault line. And during the quake that was the sixties, the earth opened, and seeing the center under all that chaos has stayed with me my entire life. In that chasm, I was able to sense the deeper, more eternal nature of things. And that deeper knowing has directed the course of my life.

I did not have a prominent role in the starburst of tensions that shed light in a dark world. I was just one of many tossed about in the helix of suffering and possibility that was our time.

You could say that my generation came of age like a bed of snails on the shore of an angry sea. Many of us were tossed about and washed away, with nothing to hold on to, while many of us hunkered down to avoid the storm, never to show our heads in public again. But some of us were slow to run or hide and, poking our heads up to see what all the fuss was about, we were caught by surprise in the churning tide that scoured us of everything we were taught. I was one of these. It was in the sixties that I truly saw for the first time. It was coming of age in the sixties that widened my circle of compassion.

This long moment of community knit our generation together before scattering us into our various lives. Years later, after marriages and countless new beginnings, we still can recognize each other by the depth in our eyes. We may be riding the subway or in a waiting room at a hospital or spilling sugar in a corner bistro. Suddenly, there is a sense of life below all our maps, and a feeling of so much to say and so few words to reach with.

Let me share one small, revealing moment from that time. More than forty years ago, I was part of a group of college students who took over an administration building in protest against so many things that we felt were oppressive. In truth, I was swept into that moment. I didn't realize what was happening. I was in deep conversation with three or four others. We were circling some elusive truth about how harsh life can be in wearing us down to our beauty, when the crowd swayed and swelled. Suddenly, like a school of fish chasing a warm spot in the current, we were in the administration building, and one of our brethren—the one too tied to his point of view to join our conversation—locked the door from the inside, stood on a desk, and declared that we had taken over the building. He was shouting about demands. Some of us cheered, while some of us groaned at having no choice. My friends and I shook our heads at how this all seemed an ironic and messy example of how life can force us to face each other.

Ultimately, I remain a student of those elemental times when the distance between us seemed less, if more strident. It's where I learned to ask so many questions. Where I learned to believe that it's the questions, entered honestly, that soften us into dropping the veil of being strangers. At times, I feel certain that the great breaking wave of that decade has crashed and rolled for forty years into the thin clarity of old men and women left in wonder with their questions. It's a happy fate for any generation: to be stripped of all cause and explanation, left with only truth and kindness, with our palms up, holding our questions like begging bowls.

I remain a student of those elemental times when the distance between us seemed less, if more strident. It's where I learned to ask so many questions.

QUESTIONS TO WALK WITH

- Ask someone older than you how the times they grew up in shaped them. In your journal, tell their story.

- Later, in conversation with a friend or loved one, tell the story of the person you listened to. Then discuss how the times you grew up in have shaped you.

33

Prosperity Blindness

The human race has had long experience and a fine tradition in surviving adversity. But we now face a task for which we have little experience, the task of surviving prosperity.

—Alan Gregg

No matter how well earned or achieved, the insulation of living well, which is different from our well-being, provides a challenge in the life of community. From the time of emperors, caesars, and monarchs, the more fortunate have sometimes held a deep compassion for the less fortunate, but more often have been blinded by the shine of their wealth from feeling the plight of others. In modern times, prosperity is more widespread. And so our tenacity in striving so hard for our own share of wealth often blinds us from seeing our connection to others.

The word "prosperity," from the Latin, means "good fortune or success, an increase in size." The word "fortune" traces back to the Old French sense of "chance or luck as a force in human affairs." Of course, none of this tells us what it actually means to be fortunate or successful, though we can see that for ages we've been preoccupied with the notion that more is better than less, and having is better than not having. Over time, a more material notion of prosperity has grown to represent a journey of gathering and having, which evokes a need to withhold and protect what we have. The more enduring notion of prosperity represents how those who have protect and guard those who do not.

In the beginning of any life, we're compelled to gather and use things to help us survive and stay engaged with life. But somewhere along the way, the things gathered solidify and wall us in. Now we're faced with surviving the wall of things that *keep* us from life. This has played out differently for each person, community, and culture throughout time. More deeply, surviving prosperity hinges on realizing when things no longer help us but hinder us. Surviving prosperity requires that we break through our wall of things and reattach ourselves to humanity.

Unaddressed, the isolation spread by prosperity can deaden our sensibilities and cause a social blindness. This is not to demonize prosperity but to acknowledge its side effects. Untreated, this isolation can weaken the heart like a resistant strain of bacteria. If ignored, the insulation of prosperity can estrange us from the unalterable fact that, as the Hindus say, *tat tvam asi,* or "thou art that"—we are each other. Once severed from this fundamental connection, we disintegrate as a people. Then self-preservation, no matter how sophisticated, takes over.

How we shun the homeless is a constant example of prosperity blindness. I'm sure you have your own stories. This one comes from my good friend Bob, who recalls the time he was drawn to follow a gay-pride parade through San Francisco, the endless colors of soul fluttering about. By the time it was done, he'd drifted into a jazz club in the Mission District. Coming out at 3 A.M., he couldn't find a cab and started walking through Dolores Park. As his eyes adjusted to the dark, he saw a carpet of bodies on the grass: leaning against the roots of old trees, spread under rusty benches, curled along crumpled fences. An unseen sea of humanity covered every available space, strewn across each other, tired, with nowhere to go.

They seemed neither dead nor alive. It was an in-between world. Suddenly, in the midst of their pain and exhaustion, Bob saw the skeletal hum of our community's underside, the brutal trail of those with everything worn away and nothing but the rawness of air between them. How do we not see this? How do we not feel this? We often pretend that brokenness happens to the unlucky, to those unable to find the wind of fortune, and yet such brokenness is our initiation into compassion. We pretend that being homeless is the individual's fault, when our insatiable want for more often presses those weakened by the journey into exile.

Whether we have more than we need or whether we're striving to get ahead, we somehow feel justified in scribing our small circle of ambition, declaring that each of us is responsible for our own fate, which is true to an extent. But in guarding what we have while striving for more, we somehow pit ourselves against each other—until one day, we slip off the wheel of prosperity, unsure how. Then we cry unfair and join the herd of those considered less. Then we're humbled to drop the catechism of fortune and wander the streets in search of help. It's often our own suffering that allows us, in time, to receive the suffering of others. Then we discover that we're responsible for our own lives *and* for each other. The health of a society depends on the compassionate braid of these two truths.

Seeing past our wall of things opens us to the suffering of others. And seeing past the glare of what we have and past our fear of losing what we have also opens us to the resilience and wisdom of those who struggle with less. Hanmin Liu of Wildflowers Institute evokes what can be termed the "wisdom of the poor." He suggests that this is an untapped source of hard-earned knowledge, which we miss entirely or rationalize because of our fear of being poor.

Consider how travel and privacy can keep us from the lessons of place and relationship. Many of us are seldom in one place long enough to cultivate the wisdom of a particular place. As well, the close-up lessons of relationship often remain out of reach for those who can afford to have a room of their own. While solitude benefits the development of the individual, having to live in the same room with others forces us to deal with conflict by developing certain relational skills—another hard-earned gift.

This is not to romanticize the difficulty of hard circumstance, but to emphasize that every circumstance offers deep learning. Obviously, there's nothing wrong with being able to travel or to have your own room. Both are blessings. More to the point, there are lessons waiting in every situation, and the wisdom inherent in not having these things is often silenced or overlooked by our fear of being without.

Those without resources can't travel and so are forced to unearth the wisdom of place, that is, they're forced to find meaning where they are—something we could all benefit from. And by virtue of their living conditions, those who struggle to make ends meet are often forced to live in close proximity with three, four, five, or more in one room, forced to unearth the more relational skills of sharing, negotiation, and compromise needed to survive—something else we could all benefit from.

The more fortunate tend to view the poor as deficient, having nothing to offer, when the human resources they possess are great and often more practiced than the rest of us. In truth, caring for the poor is more an exchange of resources than outright charity. For those who have the blessing of travel and privacy are often in need of the wisdom of place and relationship.

The painful twist of isolation arises when we start living *behind* things. As we gather and protect what we have, we find ourselves very quickly surrounded with more and more technological moats to cross in order to have simple human contact. The unexpected undertow for prospering is being separated from the rest of humanity.

In contrast, consider the longhouse tradition of the First Nations people of Canada. These were huge communal structures that would house as many as forty-eight members in an extended family. These longhouses, sometimes called bighouses, were an early form of living together with everyone in view.

I'm not advocating that we become ascetic or that we give up our homes for larger communal spaces. I'm encouraging a more heartful life through which we put people above things, regardless of what we have. For I long to inhabit the longhouse that we carry within us, so we can remember our larger family of relationships and live together with everyone in view.

Our challenge is to redefine prosperity as *an inclusive form of relationship* that not only protects us from the physical hardships of living, but that allows us to see past our fear of not having, so we can stay engaged in the well-being of each other. We don't need to discard what we have, but we do need to bring down the wall of things that keeps us from each other. As Abraham Heschel says, "To be is more essential than to have. Though we deal with things, we live in deeds."

Our tenacity in striving so hard for our own share of wealth often blinds us from seeing our connections to others.

QUESTIONS TO WALK WITH

- In your journal, describe your immediate circle of connection, your family. Then describe your next circle of connection, your friends. Then describe your third circle of connection and your openness to the experience of others. How might you widen each circle of connection?

- In conversation with a friend or loved one, tell one story of your blindness to others.

34

THE WANTING PLACE

When I see the Ten Most Wanted lists . . . I always
have this thought: If we'd made them feel wanted
earlier, they wouldn't be wanted now.

—EDDIE CANTOR

THE WRITER GEORGIA Heard asks, "What is your *querencia?*"

In Spanish, querencia describes a place where one feels
safe, a place from which one's strength of character is
drawn, a place where one feels at home. It comes from
the verb quere, which means to desire, to want . . . quere
means the wanting place.

For me, the wanting place is not a place of surface wanting—
for clothes or money or a car—but a place of relationship, a
place of yearning in which I feel my want to return to the natural element in which my soul breathes. How do we find this

place of relationship? How do we stay faithful to this place that feels like home, to which we return to heal? When was the last time you returned there? Do you still know the way?

Under all our burden and joy, this safe, interior space that feels like home is the spot of honest being that we arrive at by being who we are and by inhaling the very aliveness of things, when we risk enough to let that aliveness in.

Another name for this safe, interior space that we all long for is the Original Presence we were born with. Like salmon, we're drawn to return to our place of birth. For salmon, their place of birth is a physical location. For us, our place of birth is that Original Presence we know so freshly in the center of our being. Because we are so rearranged for being in the world, we have to return, again and again, to that Original Presence to renew our authenticity.

A moment of return happened to me the last time I was in New York City. Up early, I went to sit with the trees in Bryant Park, and I began to cry. I'm not sure why, but this is a place of return for me. I can't say how, but the bare trees, reminiscent of Paris, always seem to lean toward Eternity. The bare, lighted trees in the middle of this magnificent city give me a scent of the Original Presence I was born with. The thin, bare trees yearning for the light model what we all know—that reaching for the light is all that matters. Sitting in Bryant Park before these trees reminds me of this simple return. Sitting there awakens my need to reach for the light. For all our strategizing and problem-solving, stripping ourselves bare and reaching for what matters will restore us and make us strong enough and tender enough to see our way through.

Because we are so rearranged for being in the world, we have to return, again and again, to that Original Presence to renew our authenticity.

QUESTIONS TO WALK WITH

- In your journal, discuss your surface sense of wanting—for things, time, accomplishments, or experiences—and your deeper sense of a wanting place, a place where you feel completely at home. What's the difference between these forms of wanting?

- In conversation with a friend or loved one, describe a place you return to where you feel the Original Presence you were born with.

- When you can, return with your friend or loved one to this place where you sense your Original Presence. Sit there together and share what you feel.

35

THE CONSTANT UNFOLDING

Only whose vision can create the whole
[that person is] free into the beauty of the truth;
and strolls the axis of the universe
—love.

—E. E. CUMMINGS

IN THE TAOIST tradition, *tzu-jan* means "the constant unfolding of things." This unfailing embrace of life is as steady and forceful as the ocean. Still, the tensions of survival frequently get in the way, and we often lose touch with this larger unfolding. All the while, the enveloping Oneness draws us to inhabit and integrate the depth of our feelings, so we can experience the fact of Oneness and strengthen our connection to life.

This is what I think E. E. Cummings is speaking to in the quote that starts this chapter. He suggests that only when apprehending the dynamic aliveness of life in its totality are we free to live the one life we're given with a love that touches everything. When enlivened this way, we're like electrical transformers, sending energy across the country. When awake to our own lives and the Whole of Life, we're like spiritual transformers, emanating love and life-force wherever we go.

By our very nature, we're living conduits for energy. Yet we're so distracted by our attempts to problem-solve what falls apart that we forget our basic relationship to energy. Under all our problems is our inborn agreement to let the energy of life fill us, while working to remove whatever is blocking us from that energy. This wellspring of connection is a great resource, when we can open ourselves enough to let it fill us.

Most of the time, we labor so hard to choose a path—a way, a religion, a philosophy, a code to live by—that we seldom allow ourselves the chance to feel the wellspring of awe that resides in the living connection *between* all paths. It takes an openness of heart and mind to see where things are joined. *Glimpsing* the Whole of Life is the beginning of a deeper practice, by which we learn to *inhabit* the Whole of Life, in order to feel the power of meaning that resides in everything. In my own practice, I work very hard to feel the intersection of all these connections.

The truth is that life doesn't add up but opens up. We've been trained to think of Eternity as an endless succession of years, one unfolding after another. And so immortality has been imagined as living forever. But we experience Eternity through the moments we enter thoroughly. Through such moments, everything that ever lived and ever will floods into our being with a sense of all time and place. Being washed in this way by Eternity changes how we see, how we hear, how we feel, and how we understand the relationship of all things.

For Eternity is not abstract. Eternity is the pulse of all life in the center of every experience. When I touch this sacred but momentary awareness, I feel like a blood cell drifting in the heart, glimpsing the entire body it's in, feeling the very heart that is its home pumping around it.

The health of our being depends on this kind of awareness, in which we remember our relationship to Source, self, and each other. Indigenous traditions have always had an elder responsible for the tribe's memory, someone who serves as a keeper of the tribe's history with Wholeness. Often, this elder is the keeper of stories that detail how ancestors fell in and out of trouble, the keeper of how members of the tribe broke apart and were made whole again.

We've lost this community function, in part because, in our fear of pain and death, we've marginalized the value of elderhood. We're more intent on quarantining and disposing of our elders than learning from them. As a result, we've invoked a form of tribal amnesia with regard to humanity's history with Wholeness. One of the great challenges today is how to restore the capacity of community memory with regard to the spiritual journey.

The first and most obvious remedy is to re-establish the value and honor of elderhood. The second, more personal remedy is that we each need to become our own elder and reanimate the practice and rites of remembering ourselves into Wholeness. The knowledge and practice of how to restore Wholeness is crucial to releasing our resilience of Spirit.

Being with friends can widen our sense of Wholeness. Rich is such a friend. His gentle and endless curiosity assumes that everything is connected. Last winter I was visiting Rich, when, out of a long silence, he said, "I wonder who told the very first story and why?" This made me smile as he returned to that silence, like an old fish diving back down after gulping some air.

That night I dreamt of a prehistoric ledge where a clan had lived for generations. The grandson of the chief kept bringing him forms of tribute to show how much he loved him. He hunted a mountain lion and brought the carcass back to the ledge. He carved a knife from animal bone, engraving it for the chief. He even carved his grandfather's image on the side of the mountain.

When the grandson ran out of things to bring, the chief said, "I appreciate your thoughtfulness in all the things you bring, but you are the gift. With each kindness, you affirm the lineage we're a part of. I believe in this lineage, and I believe in you."

When I woke, I had this strong feeling that life is really just one story we each belong to. I made some coffee and sat on the porch in the morning sun, thankful to have touched the human family across the ages. Like lost children who discover, once grown, that they were never orphans, love wears away the illusion that we're unknown to each other.

Life doesn't add up but opens up.

Questions to Walk With

- In your journal, tell a story in which you experienced how life doesn't add up but opens up.

- Indigenous traditions have always had an elder responsible for the tribe's history with Wholeness. In conversation with a friend or loved one, begin to tell the story of your own history with Wholeness.

36

FOUR SMALL LESSONS

It's the small moments that save us by opening
the world.

—MN

OSKAR IS A generous friend who returns to Sweden where his
father's family still lives. He only gets to go every other year.
On his last trip, he discovered that there's a law that allows
anyone to tent in your yard or on your land for twenty-four
hours, till they can find their way. When asked, his grandfather
said, "I didn't know it was a law, but we've always done this.
Because you never know when you will lose your way." What a
beautiful lantern to leave out for strangers. What a simple way
to teach each other how to care. I look at Oskar's kind eyes as
he tells me this and realize that his open heart has a heritage.
While the mind makes borders, the heart lives below them.

* * *

BETWEEN 1934 AND 1939, Roman Vishniac took sixteen thousand photographs of Eastern European Jewish life, trying to preserve a culture he feared would be exterminated. Once aware of his efforts, the Nazis began to hunt Vishniac. They never caught him, but they did destroy over fourteen thousand of his prints. One of the prints to survive was of eleven-year-old Nettie Stub, the photo taken in 1938 in Zbaszyn, a Polish detention camp. Like pollen on the wind, her picture was somehow circulated along with several of Vishniac's Zbaszyn photographs. Later that year, Nettie was rescued and brought to safety in Sweden by the Red Cross, along with several other children. In 1983, Nettie Stub, then living in the Bronx as Nettie Katz, couldn't believe it when she saw this picture of herself as a frightened little girl in Vishniac's seminal publication *A Vanished World*. She found the photographer to thank him, for she was certain that the Red Cross chose to save her because of his photograph.

* * *

MY DEAR FRIEND, Pam, went to Lowe's to buy a sprinkler. The person waiting on her was an African American man. He asked her how she was doing, and, of all things, Pam decided to answer him honestly. She told him that she was saddened by what was happening in the world, by all the young black men being shot by police. After a while, she said that she was embarrassed by the pain her whiteness has created. Stunned, the salesman shared that he was married to a white woman and that they had a beautiful five-year-old son. He just kept saying quietly, "That's what I'm most worried about." Pam shared that she had a son and that she felt such a sorrow, knowing how different their sons' experiences would be. The two gentle souls stood in the aisle in this huge home-improvement store speaking about life the only way they could, through the eyes of their children. After a time, they shook hands and introduced themselves. They repeated their names to each other. As Pam walked away, she turned around and wanted to say something else, though she couldn't find what it was. Instead, they just smiled at each other and went back into their lives.

* * *

MY WIFE, SUSAN, was teaching pottery to four- and six-year-olds. One day, a little boy, Billy, didn't feel well. He stopped what he was doing and simply stood in the middle of the room without making a sound. Very quickly, the other little ones sensed that something was wrong. In a few minutes, the entire group encircled Billy. They were all up close showing their concern, as if being close would hold him up. After Susan tended him, she noticed that no one was moving. So she said, "Everyone is concerned about you, Billy. Can you let them know if you're alright?" Billy nodded, took a deep breath, and said, "I'm alright." Only then did the others go back to their piles of clay.

Three things stand out from this little story. First, the fact that Billy didn't hesitate to be immediate and visible with his suffering. Then the second effort could show itself: everyone held Billy up by encircling him with their concern. Finally, there was an acknowledgment that the group's concern wasn't wasted. It was all so gentle, direct, and simple. At what point in growing up do we lose these qualities? At what degree of suffering do we refind them?

* * *

WHEN OPENED ENOUGH, it's hard to tell what you carry and what I put down. When opened enough, it's hard to tell where the burden begins to lift and whose it really is. But either way, feeling each other's journey brings us to the edge of life as we know it. There, we're asked to take each breath as if it's our first and last, and to love whatever we find, as if the stranger before us is our beloved. Daring to love this deeply, we begin to give our all, as if we were born to put the world back together without any reward, like the anonymous cell that mends a broken bone.

While the mind makes borders,
the heart lives below them.

QUESTIONS TO WALK WITH

- In your journal, describe a simple kindness that changed your life.

- In conversation with a friend or loved one, tell one story of a small moment you witnessed or were a part of that opened the world.

37

OUR ORBIT OF CONCERN

There's a lot of talk in this country about the federal deficit. But I think we should talk more about our empathy deficit—the ability to put ourselves in someone else's shoes; to see the world through those who are different from us. . . . [For] we live in a culture that discourages empathy. A culture that too often tells us our principal goal in life is to be rich, thin, young, famous, safe, and entertained. A culture where those in power too often encourage these selfish impulses. . . . I hope you don't listen to this. I hope you choose to broaden, and not contract, your [orbit] of concern.

—BARACK OBAMA, JUNE 19, 2006

REPAIRING THE WORLD doesn't always mean putting up walls. Often, it means taking down walls. As you're walking through a city, any city, imagine for a moment that all the walls are gone. Suddenly, society is an open marketplace. Now you can see everyone. Now it's harder to maintain the illusion that we're alone. Now our sense of community is palpable. I'm not suggesting we remove all walls. After all, there are legitimate reasons to have walls: for shelter, safety, and privacy, to name a few.

What I'm suggesting is that for the health of our community, we imagine life without walls from time to time. Like a social X-ray, we might benefit from a yearly checkup to see what's broken or clogged or where something unhealthy is growing.

At the very least, we would see each other without impediments and remember that living together in the open is possible. We might remember that we built the walls. We put them there—or inherited them. It would help, once a year, to assess how we're living and to discern which walls are necessary and which need to be taken down.

Communism was a failed experiment at the forced removal of all walls. And the extreme of capitalism, with no regard for those around us, is proving to be just as flawed in the other direction, creating more walls than we need.

Crisis often removes the walls for us. When we can see each other so clearly in need, it is in our nature to help each other in the smallest and deepest ways, swiftly and with grace. In the aftermath of Hurricane Sandy, which devastated much of the East Coast in October 2012, my good friend Carole and her daughter Jena, who live in the West Village in New York City, opened their small apartment when it became clear they had the only landline working in the neighborhood. Carole said with ease, "We rigged up a bell to ring outside (our buzzer of course wasn't working) so people could come in and call their relatives and friends. And we had stove-top gas so we could offer a hot cup of tea or coffee."

The starkest moments sometimes beg for the softest and simplest gesture: opening a door, offering a chair, a cup of coffee, a blanket, or a rub of tired shoulders. The smallest effort of honest care can empower resilience.

The most insidious wall that keeps us from our kindness is the clear one that makes us a watcher. Often, we stand by and watch others suffer because their pain is too much like our own. Or when not in pain, we fear that opening our heart to another's pain will diminish our contentment. Yet, the bringing down of walls is the work space of compassion.

One test of our compassion is how we honor the suffering of others when we're not suffering. For while we're content and peaceful, someone else is fighting for their life, and while we're struggling with pain or loss, others are falling in love or experiencing joy. We're asked to honor the totality of life swirling about us beyond the walls we construct around our joy and sorrow. For all things are true at once, and only the depth of an open heart can let these mysteries merge within us until they release a deeper and more vital wisdom.

Yet letting all things in with exquisite empathy doesn't eliminate the need for justice or social repair, nor does it diminish the pain or joy we each feel at different times in our journey. Still, opening our heart to the plight of others matters. It's the first step toward finding our kinship with all things. Such openness of heart lets humanity know itself. Such nameless care readies us to claim our place in the human family. For today you may be blessed with the comforts of a warm bed and plenty to eat, and tomorrow you may need the kindness of a stranger. We take turns on the wheel of life: falling down and getting up, or having more than we need and then in time needing more to make it through. In this we all share the same hunger and quench the same thirst.

When our walls come down and we begin to open our heart, the apprenticeship of compassion is to feel for those we can identify with: broken heart to broken heart, loss to loss, illness to illness. But this is just the beginning, the training ground of compassion. Once we've entered the ground of our compassion, we're challenged to open our hearts to those whose suffering is outside of our experience. We're called to give our hearts over to them just because we know they're in pain, not pairing their pain with our own, not confining our compassion to the suffering that mirrors our own. This deeper form of compassion is how we grow—through loving others—beyond the limits of our personal experience.

We each have mythic moments, in which our walls come down and compassion arises, moments often waiting in the tangle of our days, moments when someone pauses to see us and speak truth to us, when someone loves us enough to hold us in our pain. I believe these moments and those who enter them are allies, ready to help us along the way. It's being truthful about our lives that puts us in the open, and compassion that lets us become allies to each other.

Each of us builds a wall. Each of us is surprised by the crisis that makes us take it down. Each of us works at the apprenticeship of compassion. We all cycle through the wall, the crisis, the opening of our heart, and the discovery of our kinship. No one has ever been you, but compassion lets us wash into each other like watercolors.

*The bringing down of walls is the
work space of compassion.*

QUESTIONS TO WALK WITH

- In your journal, describe a time when you felt compassion for someone whose experience was beyond your own. What made you open your heart in this way?

- In conversation with a friend or loved one, describe a crisis in your life that brought one of your walls down and how that changed you, and how you relate to the plight of others.

38

GLIDE, PULL, WALK, AND CARRY

ALEX WILSON, AN associate professor at the University of Saskatchewan, is part of the Opaskwayak Cree Nation, a First Nations tribe living in Northern Canada. For centuries, her tribe has lived along the Saskatchewan River Delta system, in which many lakes and smaller rivers and streams are interlaced and connected. She describes how inhabiting the connections between all things is at the heart of her tradition:

> *The place specifically where all my family is from,*
> *Pamuskatapan, means where you have to get out of*
> *the canoe and pull it along* [to make it from one
> stream to the next.] *Our family name, our clan, as it*
> *is said in English, is Wassenas, which means, "shining*
> *light from within." So there's an understanding in our*
> *lineage that we [and our journey are] connected, or*
> *related, to light.*

The light within and the pulling along of the canoe offer a useful metaphor for how the soul, the shining light within each of us, is constantly yearning to return to the greater web of interconnected streams that make up life.

Inherently, the way we do this involves letting our light within lead us to paddle our canoe as far as we can, till we have to get out of the canoe and pull it along, so we can find and enter the next stream and paddle a bit farther.

This glide, pull, walk, and carry till we can glide again describes being a spirit in a body in time on Earth, as we traverse and name all the connections in life we can inhabit. Glide, pull, walk, and carry, only to re-enter the stream—this is the path of individuation, the path of spiritual unfolding, all guided by the light within.

Being wholehearted is the chief way that we inhabit as many of the connections in life that we can. We learn as we go, and the reward for being wholehearted, which means holding nothing back, is that we get to experience the Oneness of Things. This is how we glide when fully present in the life-force that flows under everything.

And skilled as it is, the mind is a conduit. Despite how we pride ourselves on what we know, the mind doesn't contain anything. When we think of it as a container, we struggle to fill it or to keep it from overflowing. We struggle to track what it contains and imagine ourselves as keepers of all that it contains. But when we can accept that the mind at best mirrors the stream of life, then we're touched and informed by all that moves through us and humbled to be a grateful passenger. This is how we pull ourselves along in the stream of life.

Then, when brave enough to let in what is before us, the vastness of life refreshes our consciousness. In such moments, we're carriers of all that is essential. As the Zen teacher Dōgen says, we are like a leaf that carries a drop of dew in which the Universe is reflected. All of life is reflected in that one clear drop. Each time we wake, we go clear like that single drop. We could say that joy is the sensation of being a clear, lighted drop, and that truth is what we know when clear and lighted. This is how we walk, reflect, and carry our spirit through the world.

Repeatedly, we look for how to connect all things, just as members of the Opaskwayak tribe glide, pull, walk, and carry their canoes from stream to connected stream. In such moments, we do the work of spiritual portage, whereby we carry our canoe of a life from one stream to the next, crossing whatever marsh or forest lies between.

This is how life unfolds. Underground, the streams all connect. But living on Earth, we paddle as far as we can and then must carry our life to the next small shore. Glide, pull, walk, and carry. Onward we go, with no real destination, only an inborn yearning to connect all the streams.

We're here to traverse and name all the connections in life we can inhabit.

QUESTIONS TO WALK WITH

- In your journal, describe a time of spiritual portage you experienced, where you were gliding along only to hit an unexpected shore, and how you managed to get out of your canoe and pull it along to make it to the next stream.

39

Presence and Absence

Our lives are as precarious as a lamp flame
in a strong breeze.

—Nāgārjuna

I'm sitting in a winter cabin that I've returned to year after
year, sitting before the same window, waiting for the same trees
to sway when no one's looking. As if this year I might listen
better and hear more. It's in this familiar silence that I realize
that the only thing we truly have control over in this life is our
presence and our absence. We can show up or hide. We can
reach out or turn away. We can lean in or back off. We can live
with the house of all we know open so the breeze of life can
refresh us, or we can hide and dwindle behind a barricade of
opinions. And while we have to calculate danger and guard
what we love, the only true way to protect ourselves is to be so
present that our elemental being comes forth to meet the world.
This is how the elements heal the world. Light incubates. Water
irrigates. Wind lifts. The ground sprouts. And presence enjoins

whatever it touches. This is why I return to this cabin, to be lifted by that presence one more time.

While walking in the snow, I look back at the cabin and realize that when hurt, I withdraw my presence. Yet all too often, in withdrawing, I vanish when hurt rather than relocate myself. When mistreated, I don't need to hide or muffle who I am. I just need to limit my exposure to those who would hurt me.

The snow is lightly covering my face, and I can see that no matter what we face, our real challenge is not to vanish but to keep the house we call being, open. For it's only when open and present that we can be filled with the holiness that informs everything. For presence meets presence, the way water will rush to join other water.

The sun is going down. I return to the cabin and make a fire and listen to it for hours. In the absence of the noise of my life, I can see that something in us wants to make a pilgrimage of everything. As if there's always more over there. Always some truth just out of reach because of our limitations. Always the need for more air because we can't hold our breath any longer. Always more darkness to move through because we can't stay awake any longer. Always more fire to endure because we can hold our heart like a hand over the open flame of life only so long.

But here, in the stillness, it all seems much simpler. And that ever-present simplicity calls us to return to it. It doesn't matter where we return to, because we can find it anywhere. In the climb to the top of a small mountain. In a patch of heather bending to a yellow wind. Or in the shimmering sea along a coast I've always known.

The fire needs another stick, so I stoke another log and watch it flare. In the absence of all the traffic, the presence at the heart of things has risen in me again. I feel myself filling myself. It makes me see that just as we lift weights at the edge of what we can bear in order to strengthen our muscles, we need to heart-lift at the edge of what we can bear in order to strengthen our heart. As I fall asleep, the fire turns to embers.

In the morning, the sun is climbing over the tired shoulders of night, making silk of the treetops. It hasn't reached my neighbor's cabin, not yet. He's still sleeping, as I was forty minutes ago. He still thinks it's night. As did I. This is the rhythm of presence: the fullness of being alive always climbing on the shoulders of our darkness without our knowing. This is what keeps us going: the acceptance that there's light beyond our darkness, stillness beyond our pain, and a river of dream rushing toward us.

I get in my car and rejoin the tribe I'm a part of. I stop once back in the city, park, and wander a few blocks. I enter a street I've known for years and sit on a bench and meet whatever life comes my way with no attempt to name it, to judge it, to rescue it, or to push it away. I let the homeless person I see remind me of my own vulnerability. I let the bird looking for food touch the part of me that's hungry. I let the cloud about to rain touch the part of me that's cloudy. I watch the blind woman tap the sidewalk ahead of her and feel the part of me that refuses to see. I let the light on the iron bench warm the part of me so in need of light. I rise from the bench and go down another street. I'm beginning to touch the world again. Feeling present, I'm able to give warmth to those in need of warmth.

It's only when open and present that we can be filled with the holiness that informs everything.

Questions to Walk With

- In your journal, describe your struggle between simplicity and complication. What draws you into complication, and what draws you into simplicity?

- When you can, walk slowly through the streets of your town for at least thirty minutes. Do so with no destination in mind, just noting the interplay of life before you. Later, in conversation with a friend or loved one, describe what you saw and how it touched you. Focus on one small teacher you met along the way and what it said to you.

HELPING EACH OTHER STAY AWAKE

Now, I have no choice but to see with your eyes . . .
so I'm not alone, so you're not alone.

—YANNIS RITSOS

Remaking the treasure for another,
I rediscover the treasure for myself.

—MARGO MCLOUGHLIN

The teacher Sally Hare reminds us:

> We begin life physically connected to another human being. Even as we leave the uterine cocoon to move out into the world, we're connected to our birth mothers with a cord that provides everything we need to live in the outer world. The cutting of the umbilical cord literally forces our first steps in the lifelong journey between the individual and the community. We come into the world connected, and immediately enter the cycles of separation and attachment, of letting go and holding on, that mark the seasons of human life. From our first breath, we begin living into the paradoxical roles of the individual and the community.

Given this ageless dynamic, the fundamental challenge of the twenty-first century is to help each other stay awake, by being who we are and staying in relationship.

To do this, we need every single tradition. For as the sun causes every plant to grow, the one unnamable Spirit causes all forms of belief to enter the world. And just as we need all plants to have a vital incarnation of nature, we need all forms of belief to have a vital incarnation of humanity.

This acceptance of the many ways we can journey toward meaning and grace is essential to our survival as a species. The turmoil or peace of the world depends on whether we repel what is unfamiliar or treat it as our teacher. So the nature of belief is not limited to what we choose to believe in, but is more about being students of the diversity of life as manifest through relationship.

By living our life and playing our part, we hold the Universe together. To climb with a loved one to the summit of their suffering will soften our judgments and introduce us to joy. In climbing together through our pain and joy, we come to a timeless place where truth in all its forms comes to rest.

The chapters in this section speak to how kindness and suffering can bring us to that timeless place that everyone knows as home, once what is unnecessary is loved out of the way.

40

How Day Follows Night

> The hero is [the one] who is immovably centered.
> —Ralph Waldo Emerson

Often, truth speaks to me when I sleep. Perhaps because when tired, I finally drift below the tangle of the world, below the static of my mind, and even below the yearnings of my heart. So I'm up early some days, with an image that compels me, as if some part of the Universe brushes so close that its wind of aliveness wakes me. As I wake, I reach for what I see, and sometimes it forms a metaphor about the nature of life.

Today, the compelling image appeared like this: I was hovering in space, watching the Earth slowly turn in its tilt about its axis in its orbit around the sun. The Earth seemed to be letting me see the truth of its covenant with time. Hovering there in the weightless blue, I could see the Earth spin toward itself and then toward the sun, never losing touch with its center. This unstoppable turning toward itself and then toward the Source of all Light is what makes life possible. This turning toward the unknown, which appears dark, and then toward the light is what makes day follow night. And letting day follow night allows the Earth to keep its destiny, which is to orbit the sun. This spinning toward ourselves and then toward the light, never losing touch with our center, is what makes life possible for us.

I hovered there, no longer asleep but not quite awake, and I could see that the effort it takes for the Earth to carry itself is enormous and endless. I could see that—as Atlas has to hold the world on his shoulders forever, as Prometheus has to endure an eagle eating his liver and feel it heal every day, as Narcissus is hypnotized by his own reflection until he can break free of it—the Earth forever holds the weight of all life as it turns on itself. And I could see the effort it takes for us to shoulder our weight as we turn on ourselves.

Now that I'm awake, it's clear that the Earth models the balance necessary between inner and outer living. As we move through the days, we spin like the Earth away from the light and then toward the light, into ourselves and then out into the world. We spin through all kinds of weather, turning on the axis of our center, our soul, the part of us that goes nowhere. We turn inward with our being and then outward with our becoming. And this turning around a center that holds us up is how we shoulder our weight, endure our pain, and break our own reflection.

What this means for me, today, is that I need to be quiet and take things in. I need to watch the small bird chip at the ice that's covering its food, to listen to the wounded stranger tell her story to the cashier who doesn't want to hear it. I need to turn toward the silence that lets the truth of things be known again. I need to restore my personal balance between giving and receiving, because the pulsing, resting spot where they touch holds open the mysteries of life. I need to spin in balance like the Earth between my call to turn inward and my call to live in the world. Living both calls keeps the world going.

As we turn inward with our being
and then outward with our becoming,
we shoulder our weight, endure our pain,
and break our own reflection.

QUESTIONS TO WALK WITH

- In your journal, describe the condition of your spiritual balance these days. Which has more of your attention right now: turning inward or turning out into the world? Are you too far away from the fire in your center or too far away from the Source of All Light? What do you need to do right now to restore your spiritual balance: give more or receive more?

- In conversation with a friend or loved one, describe someone you know who you think is too inward. What do you perceive as their strengths and difficulties? Now describe someone you know who you think is too far out in the world. What do you perceive as their strengths and difficulties? Which of these traits apply to you?

41

Each Time I Begin

Spirit only wants for flying.
As to who does it, She only
has a passing fancy.

—Anonymous

Recently, I stood before Auguste Rodin's *The Age of Bronze*, as I have done perhaps eight times in twenty years. The statue is so lifelike that when exhibited at the 1877 Salon in Paris, Rodin was falsely accused of having made the statue by casting a living model. The figure's lids are closed, his right hand on top of his head, his mouth slightly open, his other hand just letting go, the eyes beneath his lids just about to see. This spirit about-to-be has always awakened something in me that seems to go to sleep in the throes of life, though it never leaves me. Somehow, the statue reveals the face of a soul remembering itself after great struggle. The figure is only bronze, shaped and fired by a man long dead. Yet like all great art and great truth, this statue is an unexpected mirror of the magnificence we carry and long for, unaware that it lives within us.

The hard work of living can make us forget why we're here until we're reawakened. As our eyes constrict and dilate all day long, the tangle of living collapses our awareness of all that is precious, which after a time we remember. This constriction and dilation of awareness is an inner form of day following night. And anything can cause our collapse of awareness: pain, worry, fear, illness, our over-identification with a loved one, the loss of a loved one, a sudden evaporation of purpose, or a sudden lack of worth.

After stumbling out of my first marriage, I tripped into re-membering who I am unto myself. After almost dying during my struggle with cancer, I remembered what it's like to be born. And after losing my job after sixteen years, I remembered what it's like to meet the world with nothing but my name.

Each time I began again, I was stunned to recall that we're complete as we are, about to burst into our aliveness. Like Rodin's *The Age of Bronze,* each of us is a beautiful soul just looking for ways to come alive, again and again. The soul keeps flooding through the openings we provide until we remember that we're vitally connected to all of life.

But even when the move forward was absolutely right, there was a part of me intent on pining for my old identity and my old way of life, whether it was glorious or terrible. It's natural to grieve and lament, but the questions remain: What are we grieving and what are we afraid to let go of?

Through all our hardships and entanglements, we're in a constant cycle of expansion and contraction. We gather and inhabit a self, only to fill it to the brim. Then, with no room left to grow, we're asked to empty that self so we can take in more of life. This progression of gathering and emptying lets us incorporate what we learn into a more elemental sense of self. This growing by emptying happens each time the soul remembers itself.

Paring down and becoming elemental is a hard process to grasp, because we live in a culture that is preoccupied with an expanding sense of growth, obsessed only with getting bigger, obsessed with enlarging the self and never emptying the self, which we need to do so we can take in new knowledge. For the self doesn't get its worth from what it contains, but from the life that moves through it, the way a tree or flag comes alive for the wind that moves through it. When self-reliant at all cost, we become insular and sorely out of balance, which only makes us expand like a balloon. Once tense and inflated, we begin to fear anything that might come near, afraid the slightest touch will puncture our world.

Underneath these tensions is a paradox that shapes us. For when burrowing in the ground, we lose sight of the earth; when planting the seed, we lose sight of the harvest; when feeding our hunger, we lose sight of the food; when building the next step, we lose sight of the dream; when looking up close, we lose sight of all that surrounds us; when focused on ourselves, we lose sight of others; and when living our very personal life, we lose sight of the beauty and power of the Spirit that runs through all souls.

Our purpose is not to choose between what's up close and what's far away, but to let the light of the world shine through our humanness. In spite of our habits and fears, our next ounce of aliveness takes form from immersing ourselves completely in the moment at hand, the way a cup dipped in a lake is filled with fresh water. This baptism of presence—of being bent by experience to dip the cup of our life into the water of life—fills and awakens us. This is the baptism I experience each time I'm forced to begin again. And each time my soul remembers itself, I'm asked to honor that this is the one life we're given. Though we can perish in a second, the instant of life moving through us is more than enough.

So as you feel the press of where tomorrow leads you, remember that no matter how great an opportunity awaits, it's actually leading nowhere—only opening where you are. Our soul is revealed by how experience moves through us, not where it takes us. The quiet secret is that inhabiting our humanness releases who we are, and whatever soul-presence is revealed by wriggling through the circumstances we're given can never be taken away.

These mysterious awakenings return us to ourselves. Each time we remember after forgetting, we're drawn to love the spot of grace from which our soul opens, the way a flower loves the tip of stem it opens from. And whenever the soul remembers itself, no matter how long we've been away, the spirit begins to blossom. Just as perennials bloom, wither, die, and turn to mulch, only to seed, break ground, and bloom again, the soul is a perennial that keeps breaking ground through the many chances we give it.

Growing by emptying happens each time
the soul remembers itself.

QUESTIONS TO WALK WITH

- In your journal, describe a piece of music, art, or poetry that speaks directly to your soul. What does it touch in you? Begin a conversation in your journal with that part of your soul.

- In conversation with a friend or loved one, tell the story of a time of great change for you, during which someone or something tried to persuade you not to go forward. How did this person or circumstance present itself? How did you respond?

42

The Finitudes

FINITUDE: the state or quality of having limits or bounds.

It's TAKEN more than sixty years, but I've stopped trying to figure out what people want. Now I'm working on *not* being afraid when *not* giving people what they want. Now I'm trying to absorb light, which emanating from a person feels like truth. Trying to let light pass through, which emanating between people feels like love. As I'm thinking about all this, I stumble on Martin Heidegger's notion of dwelling with care in the being that underlies everything. I feel myself saying yes, only to discover he supported Hitler and enforced Aryan law as rector of the University of Freiburg. There's a zealous telegram to Hitler. And he was vociferous in offering three *"Sieg Heils"* at the end of his inaugural address as rector. Now, not being shaped by what people want seems trivial. Or is it the DNA of conscience? Hannah Arendt, his student and lover, was a Jew. Yet she testified on his behalf after the war.

How are we to hold such contradictions? Somewhere violets are being watered in the sun, and somewhere flesh is burning. These extremes are hard enough to take in, yet how does this happen in the same person without their soul exploding? We're pragmatically taught to take what we need and leave the rest. Why not drink from Heidegger's being and push the rest away? But the pushed-away parts evolve, too. I'm trying to absorb what we've done to each other throughout history, trying to eat all of what I see and scrub one thing back to the beginning.

Often, what we know and what we do stretch in different directions. How far these drift or are torn apart determines whether we're making promises we can't keep or losing hold of an ethical life or, worse, lying to ourselves and each other. I've lived long enough to know all three. And I remember starting out, so moved and in awe of writers and teachers I deemed as masters. I remember meeting someone whose work had opened me to a deeper understanding of kindness and how disheartened I was to find him so unkind. Then I traveled to study with someone deeply skilled in acceptance only to find her completely intolerant. And when I began to teach alongside others, I remember sharing time at a conference with a renowned, gifted exemplar of mindfulness who went on for an hour longer than his allotted time—*of course, about mindfulness!*

At first I thought them hypocritical. But being humbled by the human journey, I'm not so sure. Now, when I run into such discrepancies, I wonder if some of these teachers are having a bad day. Others may be flawed pilgrims, like the rest of us, seeing something worthy to aim for but only touching it briefly from time to time. And some, for sure, are hypocritical: proposing one way of being with unfaltering conviction while giving up on living that way. Or worse, skilled at saying one thing while deliberately doing another.

Still, it seems important to know whether someone like Heidegger was having a bad day or had lost his bearings as a human being. Was he, as his defenders say, going along with the Nazi agenda to keep the University of Freiburg open and viable? Was he, like Galileo, recanting what he knew to be true, to save his own life? Sadly, there's ample evidence that he actively worked to denounce and demote Jewish faculty at the university. It's also clear that he remained a member of the Nazi Party till the end of the war, long after resigning from the university. Since Victor Farias published his book *Heidegger and Nazism* (1987), no one denies Heidegger's support of Hitler and his policies. However, philosophers continue to disagree on whether the actions of his life bear on the validity of his philosophy.

This is the quandary we're compelled to wrestle with: Does how we live validate or invalidate what we know? What's the difference between being a flawed ethical person and a cruel hypocrite? I believe how we live matters greatly. Working these questions in the crucible of our relationships seems an important way to clarify what is worth knowing and what is insidious. Just what do we learn from each other by how we treat each other? Can I find anything meaningful in Heidegger's work on being, if he was so cruel to others? And if all I knew of him was how he acted in the face of oppression and never read a word of his philosophy, what would his legacy be then? What would his life teach me about being and time?

At our best, we're carriers of wisdom, sometimes able to

grow what we carry and sometimes burdened by it. This opens another imperative question: How do we get strength from what we know? For sometimes the torch that lights our way, if held too close, can blind and burn us. And many of us are compelled to a better way, though we can never live up to it, and so always fall short of what we aspire to. For integrity resides in bringing together who we are and what we do. Though we'll never arrive at complete integrity, any more than we can ever be done with breathing.

My good friend Parker Palmer speaks of this irrevocable discrepancy between what is possible and what is real, not as something to avoid or remedy, but to live through. To be clear, Parker is not speaking about the hypocritical and dissociative gap exhibited by Heidegger, but more about the inevitable reach of our soul and our flawed aim as human beings. He sees living through this tension between our dreams and our experience as the threshold of soul work. Parker speaks of this authentic effort as *standing in the tragic gap*:

> *I would argue that the best kind of leadership and citizenship comes from educating people to stand knowingly within this tragic gap—without letting the tension between reality and possibility pull them to one pole or the other. When we are pulled too far to the side of "reality" we become disengaged cynics, and when we are pulled too far to the side of "possibility" we become irrelevant idealists.*

What if the work we avoid but can't escape is not to go anywhere—not forward or to greater heights—but to devote ourselves to bringing who we are and what we do closer together? What if the hardest, most necessary task is to have all that we know *enliven our care,* until we pour the dream like a salve of honey into every flaw and break we find?

Integrity resides in bringing together who we are and what we do. Though we'll never arrive at complete integrity, any more than we can ever be done with breathing.

QUESTIONS TO WALK WITH

- In your journal, describe someone you admire for their integrity. Then describe someone you know to be wise but who can't seem to live according to what they know. Finally, describe someone you feel is not integral. What in your mind makes the first admirable, the second well-intentioned, and the third hypocritical? What do these people have in common? What separates them?

- In conversation with a friend or loved one, discuss your own range of integrity, sharing a story of when you were in full integrity, then another story of when you were well-intentioned but unable to live according to what you know. Finally, share a story of when you found yourself being hypocritical. Describe what conditions led you to each position.

43

Sweet Teachers

I HAD MET Ernie and Cathy several years ago, two sensitive souls who lived in Victoria on Vancouver Island in British Columbia. A few years ago, their lives were thrown into a difficult depth, as an inoperable brain tumor made Ernie's light more simple and bare. And Cathy stayed near him, loving his strong blue flame.

They chose to live this part of their lives openly, somehow knowing that just as fire needs oxygen, the heart, no matter what it's asked to face, needs the open air of relationship to keep going. I admired them both.

Before Ernie died, he recommended a wise and touching book, *Ten Thousand Joys and Ten Thousand Sorrows,* by Olivia Ames Hoblitzelle. The book chronicles the last days of Olivia's husband and their journey with his Alzheimer's. In the book, there's a chapter called "The Grace of Diminishment."

The notion of grace coming from diminishment is a hard door of wisdom to open. For the diminishments we face have a life of their own, which can be dark, even blinding. I know from my own journey that limitations, hard as they are to accept, bring quiet freedoms. Unable to move after surgery, I was forced to see all of life in the inch before me. Unable to hear, I was forced to make a teacher of silence. And when unable to be with my father who was dying, my heart was forced to find him in the kindness of everyone I met.

Ernie shared this moment of diminishment and the grace it opened, while walking his dogs:

> *This morning I again walked up the eight flights of stairs (yes, our elevator is out) after taking the dogs for our morning sojourn. As each day goes by, it's getting harder for our older dog (Reilly, close to fourteen) to make the climb. With each floor, I pause, sit with the younger (Kipper, he's seven), and wait. Reilly looks up from the bottom of the stairs. . . . Kipper lays down, rests his head, and looks down at his older brother. Slowly Reilly elegantly brings himself up the stairs. . . . when he reaches the top, Kipper raises his head, they look, touch, stand together, and we begin again.*

Isn't this what our lives are finally opened to: making the climb, a bit at a time, and waiting for each other along the way? Isn't this all we can hope for—to look, touch, stand together, and begin again?

When our dog-child Mira was twelve and a half, we knew the slow climb well, tender and heart-breaking with each step. When my father was bedridden at ninety-three, his arm fit like a slim branch in my palm. As he stared into my eyes from the edge of Eternity, he wondered why everything looked so soft.

And today, the rain is fine, a steady mist that enables us to go on. All of it an unexpected blessing, as are you as you read this, though you may not know it. So wait for me when the wind throws something in my eye. Then I'll wait for you when something in the shadow cast over the willow takes the wind out of your heart, because it reminds you of another time that can't be relived.

Being opened is the most difficult and rewarding part of being human. Often, this happens through our experience of less, not more. For all we learn by reaching, we learn as much when forced to be where we are. How still the trees are, rooted in one place for years, and yet they grow.

Being opened is the most difficult and
rewarding part of being human.

QUESTIONS TO WALK WITH

- In your journal, describe a tree you've seen grow over time. How has it matured and changed? If that tree were a person, how would you describe its character? What does this tree say to you about living in the open?

- In conversation with a friend or loved one, tell the story of a time when someone waited for you and what that offering of patience felt like. What did the person who waited for you teach you?

44

THE GREATER PRAYER OF BEING

In Quakerism, whatever you believe needs to be
grounded in the evidence of your own life. . . . In
Quakerism, [there's an] insistence that everyone has
within himself or herself a source of truth—an inner
light or inner teacher. . . . Of course, truth is not
the only thing we hear from within. We also hear
the voices of ego, of fear, of greed, of depression. So
Quakerism puts an equal emphasis on the role of
community in helping people sort out what they're
hearing.

—PARKER PALMER

EACH OF US walks about in a cloud of affections: our love, our
pain, our desires, our history. Then we need help from each
other to outwait the cloud, so we can regain our direct experience of life. We need to break the trance of what we want or
wish for or regret. No matter what life gives us, the task is not
to replay what we go through, but to integrate what enters our

heart. Not to linger in what might have been or what has fallen short, but to make the most of what's before us. The challenge is to feel what's real while it's real.

And we each need help sorting what we're hearing. For fear and worry are dark spiders constantly weaving webs in the corners of our mind, till one day we walk into those webs, surprised and entangled. This is why we have to still our mind and open our heart: to clean out the webs of fear and worry. Otherwise, a dark gauze grows between us and life. So just as we need to dust our home, we need an inner practice to dust our mind of all the webs we spin.

When overwhelmed by worry, fear, or regret, we start to disempower where we are, by imagining that somewhere else is better. The urban dictionary offers a contemporary expression of this painful yearning, the word *fomo,* which is an acronym for "fear of missing out." This is considered a symptom of technological withdrawal, a state of anxiety that arises from feeling bereft, and even panicked, at not having access to the internet, to calls or texts, to Facebook or Twitter. This is a modern expression of the underlying sense that humans have struggled with forever: that life is happening without us. This perilous inner state arises from investing our being in the hope that, "If I could only get over there, then life would be worth living."

But when we can sort what we're hearing and outwait the cloud of our affections, we land in the beautiful if gritty terrain of where we are. Once grounded enough to meet what is with our care, then I can love you. And the depth of that love dissolves images of life being "over there." Then my grounded sense of self starts to let others in, so that when you're in pain, I'm in pain. And when you're overflowing with wonder, I'm saturated with that wonder. This is how life grows and joins, a pain at a time, a wonder at a time—despite our clouds of affection, our webs of worry, and our fear of missing out. This is the greater prayer of being: how we grow where we are, only to dissolve through our compassion into a greater union with the life around us.

This brings to mind the story of two sisters who were very close and very competitive. Lisa, the older, was obsessed with being exceptional. She needed to excel in everything. Gail, the younger, was obsessed with experience. She needed to meet as much of life as she could. Gail would question Lisa, "Why all the work to make things happen?" And Lisa would question Gail, "Will you ever accomplish anything?" They never really understood each other, though they secretly envied each other's devotion. It was later in life, after many years apart, that Lisa fell ill and Gail came to care for her. Forced by her illness to be still, Lisa could no longer accomplish anything. It made her feel lost, but her limitations opened her to her deeper self. And forced by her love for Lisa, Gail had to become competent in her care, accomplishing a great deal from day to day. It was the fragility of life that stopped Lisa and Gail from insisting on the face each showed the world. They met in the quiet moments of one caring for the other.

Each of us is scoured over time, though we hate the scouring, hollowed to something beautiful, though we fear the hollowing. Each of us is hovered over by unseen angels and demons who want our attention. Each of us worn to a small chamber in which what matters can be heard despite the noise we make while running to and from. This scouring by angels and hollowing by demons is how we're refined while here, no matter how clouded and lost we may get along the way.

Just the other day, I was trying to outwait the cloud of my own affections. The January sun was splaying through the anatomy of trees. My dog was sniffing about, scenting mice gone underground. The only noise was the snort of her nose in snow. I was drawn again to the bare tops of trees, thinner than the rest. Drawn to the life of the tree moving all that way from its gnarly, buried root, stretching up the trunk, and twisting through the limbs, to its most exposed gesture reaching to the sky.

Then I could see that, like the length of a mature tree, from root to leafless tip, this is how we establish ourselves in the world. The deeper our roots, the higher we can reach. Now I wonder, if trees could talk, would they tell us that their roots feel the wind from the sky and that their uppermost twigs feel the earth packed around their roots?

When taking root where we are and reaching toward the light, we too feel everything all the way through. The clouds go drifting by, more visible because of the windblown twigs, just as the Truth of the Universe is more visible when we are fully here.

This is the greater prayer of being: how we grow where we are, only to dissolve through our compassion into a greater union with the life around us.

Questions to Walk With

- In your journal, describe one fear or worry that has spun a cobweb in the corner of your mind. How might you sweep it away?

- In conversation with a friend or loved one, describe a time when your love for another began to dissolve your singular sense of self and how you grew for this experience of love.

45

AN INNER RIGHT-OF-WAY

WHILE HIKING IN England, a dear friend learned that if a path is walked at least once a year, it becomes by law a public path and must be cared for and kept open, maintained by the community. This is an inspired law. For the basis of public right-of-way rests on two assumptions. First, that what one seeker learns, even by traveling once, is important to all. And secondly, that it's necessary to use a path for it to reveal its lessons. This public right-of-way evokes an *inner right-of-way*, where what one soul learns, everyone has a right to. And if you or I uncover a worthwhile path, it's everyone's responsibility to maintain it and keep it open.

The poet Henk Brandt speaks of "intimacy as the proving ground for the conscious heart." He suggests that the experiential ground of love is the heart-laboratory in which the dynamics of community are forged and tested. This too evokes an inner right-of-way, where what we learn in relationship, everyone has a right to. If blessed, we can ripple our moments of honest caring into larger and larger circles of relationship, the way fish breaking surface create ripples in a lake. By living one experience at a time, we can affect our sense of family, friendship, community, even our sense of nation and world.

Here are three examples of an inner right-of-way, where what one soul has learned, everyone has a right to. George Nakashima (1905–1990) was a master woodworker, a Japanese American born in Spokane, Washington. During World War II, he, his wife, and their infant daughter were sent to a Japanese internment camp near Twin Falls, Idaho. In that hellish place, he met Gentaro Hikogawa, an elderly Japanese carpenter who taught him the craft of woodworking.

After the war, Nakashima became an architect who worked in Paris, Tokyo, and India. All of this was an unforeseen apprenticeship to his eventual mastery in furniture design. He developed a belief that each piece of wood has a particular character hidden in the warp and crack of its grain. By carving and shaping the wood to its natural openings, it was his hope to give each piece of wood "a second life." Rather than covering up what others saw as the wood's imperfections, Nakashima showcased them.

It's a profound lesson that his own hardships led him to this all-embracing understanding of art. It's more than ironic that in his unjust internment he met his teacher and uncovered his calling. The master carver came to see the wood's imperfections as the source of its beauty.

Nakashima went on to become a master of wood joinery, especially in the techniques of dovetail, butterfly, and tenon joinery. The advantage of wood joinery is that it increases the strength and flexibility of the wood where it's joined. It's the same with relationships. We're stronger and more flexible where we're joined. And regardless of how we're taught to denigrate where we're broken, our beauty rises from our imperfections. Our strength, flexibility, and beauty come *from* our humanness.

The inner right-of-way that comes from the life of George Nakashima is that lightness and strength can rise from darkness and oppression.

The second example comes from my conversation with the Abenake elder Joseph Bruchac. He shared the simple lesson inherent in how the Diné (the Navajo) teach their children to care for flocks of sheep. In the western way, the aim is to herd and direct animals. As endless movies of the Wild West depict, a "man's man" steers the wild horses through ancient canyons, so the stallions can be tamed and bred. While less dramatic, the western approach is basically the same with sheep.

In contrast, the first thing the Diné teach is the sanctity of all creatures. From here, children are taught to go into the middle of the flock in order to establish a relationship with the sheep. Once that is done, the flock regards the shepherd as another sheep. Now there's no need to corral and herd, as the sheep will simply stay in relationship to the shepherd and go wherever the shepherd goes.

The inner right-of-way expressed here is that when treating everything as sacred, we don't have to whip and herd each other. We only have to go to the middle of our flock and wait.

The third example comes from the "Farewell" Symphony of Austrian composer Joseph Haydn. Haydn led the court orchestra for the Austrian Nikolaus I, Prince Esterházy, who so loved to be surrounded by music that he worked his court orchestra with no compassion for their hardships. In the summer of

1772, the orchestra accompanied the prince to his summer palace in Eszterháza, leaving their families back home in Eisenstadt. After an extended stay, the musicians were growing homesick and weary.

Since the prince was not approachable, Haydn composed the last movement of the symphony so that the musicians themselves would exit after playing their final passages, hoping his patron would see the obvious and let his musicians go home.

It was a mild summer night when Haydn conducted the symphony for the prince, who was brought into a reverie. Then, during the final adagio, each musician in turn played his final note, snuffed out the candle on his music stand, and left. First the oboe and second horn, then the bassoon, second oboe, and first horn. The prince felt them leave and opened his eyes. Then the double bass and cello left. The prince sat up straight, feeling the loss of the music as each musician vanished. At the end, two soft violins remained, played by Haydn himself and his concertmaster, Alois Luigi Tomasini. The next morning Prince Nikolaus sent Haydn word that the court and its orchestra would be returning to Eisenstadt that day.

There is something steadfast and telling about Haydn's soft genius. Rather than plead for his musicians, he let the power and presence of their music speak. The inner right-of-way uncovered by Joseph Haydn is the power of our presence, to be who we are until we're heard.

Whether we learn the art of joinery while being held captive, or are sent as children into the center of a flock of sheep, or snuff candles with the music of violins, when we share what we learn, we find ourselves like travelers who survive a storm, only to land on some battered shore at night. Once there, we no longer quibble over our names for the stars. We simply nod to where we've been and agree to find our way by the same nameless light we see above us.

The public right-of-way evokes an inner right-of-way, where what one soul learns, everyone has a right to.

QUESTIONS TO WALK WITH

- In your journal, describe a path you've explored that you want to share with others. Have you shared this path? If so, with who? If not, why not?

- If intimacy is the heart-laboratory for the dynamics of community, enter a conversation with a friend or loved one and describe one thing you've learned from your own work at intimacy that speaks to the nature of all relationship.

46

HELPING EACH OTHER STAY AWAKE

> We must survive the night come what may.
> And the only way to survive the night is to
> affirm authenticity, personhood, and people.
>
> —JOEL ELKES

As I TRAVEL to offer workshops and retreats, I enter a depth with willing others who've been opened and shaped by life. Through that depth, we create a path to what matters by which we enter the temple that is the world. I remain humbled and excited by the mystical fact that, try as we do, this depth can't be opened alone. We need each other to do this, even though no one can experience life for you. And so we journey as pilgrims of the heart, alone and together, crossing this threshold of depth whenever we dare to tell the truth of our lives.

I open these gatherings by admitting that I have no answers and that we're here to compare notes, because no one knows how to navigate the mystery of being alive. I then try to open a heart space through which we can enter the realm of all that matters, which is always waiting just below the interruptions of life. When followed beyond our wants and fears, what matters will lead us to the bareness of being that informs all life. I open this heart space by reading poems, telling stories, and sharing metaphors that reveal the unseeable architecture of existence.

I remind everyone that gathering like this is part of a lineage that goes back to the earliest of times. For when winded by fear or pain or stalled by clarity or inexplicable beauty, human beings have always stopped to gather, to try to make sense of things. I imagine in prehistoric times, after outrunning a mountain lion, after dragging the one member of the clan maimed by the lion back into their cave, they all assembled, out of breath, to ask each other, "Is this all there is? What are we doing here? Is there any meaning or sense to all this?"

And while we need to pause to look at life and what it does to us, while what we discover by looking into our experience together is helpful, we're always thrown back into life, where everything is of a whole: beautifully tangled and enmeshed in a numinous aggregate of shimmering forces that lift us up and knock us down repeatedly.

So my job when entering these gatherings is to start more things than we can finish, so that the space of our gathering and the relentless stream of life happening outside of our time together are understood and accepted as one. Our job is to help each other remember that pausing to make sense of life—whether in a cave or workshop or sangha or temple or church or a university class-room or in the belly of the night with a dear, trusted friend—pausing to gather like this is a resource and not a refuge.

I'm heartened by the tradition of Native American elder councils, which always meet in circle. Not just for equity, as there is no head to a circle, but so that each person has a direct view of the Center. The sacred assumption is that we need everyone's view of the Center to grasp it. We need everyone's view of the Center to open it. We need to listen to everyone's view and put our meanings together in order to enter the temple that is the world. And so the need to gather meaning, not choose it.

When we can come together like this—ensuring everyone has a direct view of the Center, honoring our deepest conversations as a resource and not a refuge, when we can open a heart space between us and enter the depth of life, all to share the truth of our lives—then the teacher moves around the room. Then the wisdom of an open heart appears here and there, revealing a deeper mosaic of truth that no one person can surface alone. In moments like this, our stories cure into a remedy that anyone can drink. As a teacher, my hope is to step aside so everyone can be their own teacher, so that everyone can be their own remedy.

During the last year, I've gathered with hundreds of people, good souls living tenderly and resiliently through their rough and ordinary days. In Connecticut, the teacher appeared as a mother who felt vacant of love as she tumbled from bad relationship to bad relationship. Her son is a heroin addict who tried to kill himself after desperately feeling lost. On the way to the hospital, she kept asking herself, "What can be so bad that you would try to kill yourself?" But in the ER, behind a gray curtain, when looking deeper into her son's eyes than she had ever looked, she saw herself. Stunned, she cried and took his hands, only to see her hands. She looked around at the rest of us and said, "From that day, a veil that had kept me from life was torn apart, and a veil that had kept me from my son was pulled aside. Yellows are more yellow now, pain is hard but clear, and when I touch my son, I feel this being who came through me into the world."

In Seattle, the teacher appeared as a quiet dentist, who, after years of removing decay from others, after years of softening their pain, saw a deer come up to his window while he was filing down a crown. It stared at him and he began to well up. The deer leapt away, as if taking a cloud from his heart, and he suddenly felt completely alive. In our group, he went quiet, then said, "Speaking and listening from the heart clears the fog."

In Santa Barbara, a grade-school nurse was the teacher. She asked, through her tears, "Why?" after telling us that her sister-in-law set herself on fire. All we could do was lean toward her, bearing witness to the fire in her heart that she can't put out. All we could do was hold her with a kind silence and listen to the lessons of that fire.

In New York City, a fireman was the teacher. He cares for his aging aunt, who told him the other day that she's been looking for something for a long, long time and she just found it. It was there all the time. But she wouldn't tell him what it is. She just said, "You'll have to find it for yourself."

And in Vancouver, a lawyer who defends inmates on death row was the teacher. She said she carries them with her everywhere, especially their faces at the end. On the way to our retreat, she was stuck in the airport with more than a hundred people, when she saw her dead convicts among the living and held them as the living angels that they are. She said, "When I saw how precious and irreplaceable everyone is, I fell to my knees near my gate. Someone nearby came over and asked if I was alright. I took his hand and confessed, 'I've never been better.'"

Meeting like this is always an unexpected blessing. When

we show up like this, we help each other stay awake. When we hold each other's pain, we knit together into a net that catches truth. When we dare to let life move through us, though we don't know what it means, we enter the temple that is the world. It doesn't get any better than this.

When we can open a heart space between us and enter the depth of life, all to share the truth of our lives—then the teacher moves around the room.

Questions to Walk With

- In your journal, describe an event between you and another that you wouldn't have willingly opened. How did you enter this depth? What did this unexpected depth do to you and your relationship with this person?

- In conversation with a friend or loved one, discuss where you feel most able to look at what life does to you. It might be an internal space or an external space. When was the last time you entered this space? What keeps you from going there?

47

WITHOUT WORDS

SHE WAS BORN in northern India and has spent much of her life in Tanzania where she is living as an elder with children around the world. At eighty-two, she suffers from severe rheumatoid arthritis and has been falling more deeply into a chasm of fear. One of her sons, Pindey, lives in southern California. He has been practicing massage for over thirty years. I see Pindey twice a year when I go to teach at Pine Manor retreat center in Lake Elsinore, a spiritual oasis in the hills. It's important to pause here to say what a wise, gentle, and humble man Pindey is. But that doesn't quite reach his essence either. He is a conduit for all that is greater than us. He is a master at what he does, but it's more than technique. The skill in his hands is guided by his large heart, which allows the Well of Spirit to flow through him. And so, his touch is both calming and healing. His wisdom is in his touch.

On this brisk November morning, Pindey tells me that during the summer he felt a strong pull to visit his mother in

Tanzania. Their road together had been difficult through the years. And now, there was such a strong rush of Spirit that said she needed him. So he cleared his obligations and made arrangements to go, and off he went to Tanzania to find his mother one more time.

Pindey's native tongue is Punjabi, but he converses with his mother in Swahili. He tells me that there are many words in Punjabi that can't quite be said in English. Just as there are many compelling forces that call us which have no names.

It took Pindey twenty-two hours to fly from LA to Nairobi and then a few more hours to his mother's side. Then he sat with her day after day—for a month—just holding her. When she would wake in the night consumed with fear, he'd hold her head until she calmed. When she'd wake in the morning in pain, he'd hold her and rock her until she calmed. He called on his years of mastery to love her without waver and without any talk of their history of difficulty. He simply stayed by her side and held her constantly. He'd sit and hold her when the nurses came and rock her long after the nurses left. When others said, "You have to rest," he thought, *This is how I rest.* When others said, "You have to go home," he thought, *I am home.* When others, meaning well, said, "You can't save her," he thought, *But she can save me.* And after thirty days, with no words, her heart had softened and, mysteriously, she began to heal. She seemed more reachable than Pindey could remember and was overflowing with gratitude, unsure how she could ever repay her son for never letting her go.

At this, Pindey wells up and says, "And *she's* asking how to repay *me.*" He shakes his head like a bird lifting into the open after a storm. This story brings into view a profound lesson that arrives without words and yet, I am left with only words to convey it. Holding is one of the great medicines. Many of us will resist holding or being held for more than a minute and yet this strong-gentle son, who has daughters of his own, had the courage to travel almost ten thousand miles to offer his relentless care to another, day and night, for a month, with no expectation. And all that giving somehow made his mother well and him stronger.

So, regardless of what problem tangles your mind, regardless of what history impinges on your sense of worth, regardless of what seems insurmountable, we can cut through the tangle that living wraps us in, if we dare to hold each other longer than we think possible until our very nature transforms our condition. For touch heals. Holding transforms. And gratitude keeps us alive and within each other's reach.

There are many compelling forces that call us which have no names.

QUESTIONS TO WALK WITH

- Describe a time when you were held deeply and how that impacted your well-being. What enabled this loved one to give so much and what enabled you to receive so much? Even if this person is aware of your gratitude, tell their story to them, again, as well as to someone else.

- In conversation with a friend or loved one, discuss a person in your life who might benefit from you holding them deeply. What is keeping you from doing this? What step can you take to offer them your care? What risk can you take to deepen your willingness to hold and be held?

48

What If?

Who looks outside, dreams; who looks inside, awakes.
—CARL JUNG

WE ALL EXPERIENCE the cycle of dreaming and waking. There's nothing wrong with either of these states. Yet each can be dangerous if used to hide from the truth. When we dream as a way to transcend or escape reality, it begins to drain our life-force. When we hide within our inwardness, avoiding the world, this too can be crippling.

My own journey with dreaming and waking has evolved over decades. I began with the dream of becoming a great writer, as if burying myself in that creative journey would lift me out of my lack of self-worth burnished in the fire of my youth. But cancer in my thirties cracked me wide open, scattering my insecure habits. I got back up and enlisted a stubbornness to pick up where I'd left off, only to have my devotion to writing unravel into a tenderness for life. This vulnerability uncovered the truth of life wherever I would go.

In time, the impetus for my dream evaporated into a wakefulness that kept landing me in the unexpected wonder of life.

Despite my attempts to get back on my dream train, I discovered that the purpose of any dream is to exercise the heart
until it awakens. And with an awakened heart, we can better
live life on Earth. When vulnerable and working to better
things, dreaming and waking are beautifully one.

The great romantic poet Samuel Taylor Coleridge (1772–
1834) speaks to the Great Unity of dreaming and waking in his
magical poem "What Then?"

> *What if you slept?*
> *And what if,*
> *In your sleep*
> *You dreamed?*
> *And what if,*
> *In your dream,*
> *You went to Heaven*
> *And there plucked*
> *A strange and*
> *Beautiful flower?*
> *And what if,*
> *When you awoke,*
> *You had the flower*
> *In your hand?*
>
> *Ah . . . what then?*

Coleridge opens the unexpected moment when dreaming
and waking become one, when the dream is in our hand the

moment we're fully here. And only the courage to be completely who we are can bring what lives within us out into the world.

Still, we're constantly challenged whether to live for today or tomorrow. I was recently asked what's on my bucket list. I dropped my shoulders and smiled to admit I don't have a bucket list—because dreaming has given way to waking. It doesn't mean I don't plan or work toward goals. I'm working right now toward my dream of finishing this book. But I've learned along the way that it's our immersion in the inquiry that is the dream dreaming itself. Life in its majesty is everywhere, so there's nowhere to go. Everything is delicious and all obstacles are teachers. Still, none of this preempts the labor of our journey.

The other day I was feeling a bit bruised and tender, confused again about what's next, yet so clear about what is. Then I chanced to read Coleridge's poem again. It made me walk into our yard and stare at a flower almost in bloom. It rained the night before, and the flower had small drops of water on the inside and outside of its petals. It swayed gently in the morning breeze. It was so delicate and yet it didn't break. It felt like a mirror of my beat-up heart.

I felt compelled to touch one of the petals. I had to kneel to look at it closely. I realized that when the petal opening feels the nectar at its center, and the center of the flower feels its petal opening, the flower is at peace. In just this way, when my dream, so intent on opening tomorrow, feels the center of my soul opening into now, my heart is at peace. Then I'm waking in my dream with the strange, beautiful flower in my hand. Ah, what now?

*The purpose of any dream is to exercise
the heart until it awakens.*

QUESTIONS TO WALK WITH

- In your journal, describe how you experience dreaming and waking. What does each feel like? What does each demand of you? What does each give you?

- In conversation with a friend or loved one, describe one thing you want in your life that you feel you need to work toward, and one thing within you that you feel you need to awaken to. What steps can you take to move closer to each?

49

TRY, ACCEPT, BEGIN AGAIN

> When an imperative arises and it has your name on
> it—it calls you and you know it's yours—take it,
> claim it, and let yourself be claimed by it.
> —TAMI SIMON

WHEN WE CAN resist the urge to compare ourselves to others or
to the imagined perfection of our dreams, our worth waits to
be revealed through the daily experience of authentic presence.
Only when this real can we discover the gifts we've carried
since birth that no one else can love into being. Though it's
never easy.

Leonardo da Vinci and Claude Monet are two dramatic examples of souls who gathered strength from what they knew as
they rode the wave of life. Both worked very hard to align their
gifts with the greater life around them. Sadly, Van Gogh was a
tragic example of someone who had the wave crash harshly over
him. Sylvia Plath and Anne Sexton were as tragic, both talented

poets who committed suicide. And Beethoven was someone who rode the wave of life, only to fall and almost drown. Yet through a tremendous effort of heart, he caught the wave a second time, riding it into his tsunami of unprecedented music. It's humbling to realize how easily we can be thrust into any of these positions, as there's only a hair's width of consciousness and circumstance between riding the wave and drowning in it.

These legendary figures highlight a journey we're all born into: we never stop paddling in the larger sea, while being tossed about by the tides of life. That we're constantly disturbed and rearranged is inherent to life's journey. The work of integrity is to somehow sustain the elements of our true nature while being disturbed and rearranged by life.

We can't explore effort very long without talking about our will. Being willful describes our insistence to make things happen, our pushing to manifest things, our constant drive toward what we imagine or aspire to. This differs from being attentive, which describes our devotion to let, and even help, things unfold. When willful, we invent; when attentive, we discover. Yet, like light and dark, or music and silence, or X and Y chromosomes, there's nothing inherently wrong with being willful or being attentive. We're born with both capacities, and they work in infinite combination.

So a basic question to ask as we summon our will is: Am I pushing things or tending things? While pushing sometimes leads to great achievements, attending leads to great experiences. Ironically, pushing often rushes us out of the holy center of our endeavor, while attending anything authentically can bring us further into that center.

And after years of pushing and tending, we might come to accept that our work is to be thorough. For in loving and creating, all we can do is receive each other completely. We are empty in the beginning and empty in the end. Neither is sad. To be thorough and emptied is our purpose. After being battered about by our endless want, we're asked to reach with whatever heart is left in a thorough attempt to accept everything. Awake in the world, we can only try.

We're all possible and limited, like a flag enlivened by the wind, though it can never be the wind. And though we're born with a yearning to see and touch everything, we can only be enlivened by what stills our heart. Though we have a need to dive into the depth of life, we have to breathe in the world. Though we're somehow bursting with a want to be great, we're forced to accept that the blessing is released when we're utterly who and what we are. And through it all, it takes a quiet courage to wake to all there is and begin again. Perhaps this is what makes the human journey noble: that we reach for everything and land where we are—that we try, accept, and begin again.

After being battered about by our endless want, we're asked to reach with whatever heart is left in a thorough attempt to accept everything.

Questions to Walk With

- In conversation with a friend or loved one, describe some endeavor you've been called to try, to accept, and to begin again. How has your commitment to this process affected you? What have you learned from staying with it?

50

The Fragrant Cliff

AFRAID OF DYING, Emperor Su Tsung of the Tang dynasty asked the great teacher Chung Hui, "After you die, what will you need?" Like a mirror held up to my soul, this question won't leave me be. I've been carrying it everywhere.

A few days ago, I stood near a large willow after a short, fierce rain. I watched the rain pool around the tree's roots with a clarity that only appears after a storm. With the smell of rain still in the air, I asked myself, "After you stop dying *here,* what will you need?" My mind said, "Nothing." My heart uttered, "Love."

This is our fate: to navigate between nothing and love. Over time, living forms a cataract over our being, which only opening the heart removes. Being alive demands that we accept this filming and cleansing as the weather of experience. Such inner weather is inevitable. But we don't solve weather, we live through it.

In addition to the filming of experience, we endlessly struggle with the layering of veils. Pain, loss, doubt, hesitation, and resignation, if untended, create veils. Any one feeling or mood that dominates our life is such a veil. Though the appearance of veils is not always of our doing. However it happens, removing ourselves from life creates a veil that dampens the intensity of living. Whether we create the veil or not, to muffle the miracle that is always present is to die to life.

And in addition to the filming of experience and the layering of veils, we all have cuts that crimp the heart. So how do we reach where we are scarred? This is the work of inner freedom. When under the press of our scars, there is no end to what we need. Once we face the them, we need only the day and each other.

And so I need more courage in being who I am everywhere. Now the question evolves, "After you die to your wounds and veils, what will you need?" I only know that the more my heart opens, the more courage reveals itself as bare and complete presence. A flower can dream of blossoming before it opens, but once opened, it stops dreaming and simply flowers. In this way, we dream of courage before the heart opens. Once fully present, we simply are.

Hundreds of years ago, a ruler afraid of dying asked his teacher, "After you die, what will you need?" It's a conversation each of us needs to have, if we are to experience the depth of life. As I approach dying, I think I will need to accept the dissolving of my self, so I can let go as I join everything. As I approach living, I think I will need the patience of soil waiting for rain, so I can feel the aliveness of everything fill me. And after I stop dying *here,* I think I will need the very same openness and patience to be fully alive.

The fragrant cliff is any moment where, briefly and deeply, we stop dying to life. In that recurring sweetness, the wounds we carry, the ones we stitch from so many legitimate hurts, begin to heal. And the veils that accrue like weather are parted. And for the moment we are cleansed—our being, heart, and mind allowed to breathe in unison. The fragrant cliff is where we climb into the open and live, dusting our hearts off as we stand before Eternity, vulnerable and empowered, in awe and grateful that, at last, there is nowhere else to go.

Over time, living forms a cataract over our being, which only opening the heart removes.

QUESTIONS TO WALK WITH

- In your journal, explore this question for yourself, "After you stop dying here, what will you need?"

- In conversation with a friend or loved one, describe one veil that has been parted in your life. How did this veil come to be, and how did it come to be parted?

51

THE AGENTS OF KINDNESS

What keeps buildings and forests, rocks and oceans
from flying off the planet and spinning into space?
What keeps the elements that make up people and
animals from ungluing? A physicist would use
mathematical equations to prove to you that gravity
and electromagnetism hold the universe in place. But
what came before them? What came first? Love. Love
came first.

—ELIZABETH LESSER

IT'S THE SILKEN threads of care woven through the brutal
storms of time that hold everything together. A loved one's
picture carried through a war and delivered to a grandchild
thirty years later. The seed that isn't washed away that takes
root, arriving in the world as an orchid, whose beauty makes a
young girl become a painter. The memory of the moment we
met twenty-five years ago overwhelming me as I watch you
sleep this morning. The laughter of my father while planing a

piece of mahogany, which kept me believing in the love of work and the work of love while going through cancer. These silken threads are everywhere—a web of barely visible connections that infuse us with resilience when we're forced or loved to find our way through what we're given.

In the midst of great turmoil, in the cascade of human catastrophes, these threads of care seem obsolete—artifacts of a gentler time. But they wait under all the breakage that overcomes us. These fine threads of care can be lost but never broken. They wait for the devotion of a single soul, daring to stand up for life in the midst of cruelty, daring to love everyone in the face of prejudice, daring to step out of the drama that says we're strangers or enemies, daring to help those in hiding come out into the open. One silken thread of care held on to and followed, sometimes for years, can repair the world.

It was my grandmother who taught me to be kind, who, with the weary faith of a sturdy immigrant, taught me that life opens for those who dare to give. Once living in the open, there is no career but being kind.

So let's keep each other company, which means let's be companions, which goes back to the French, meaning "one who breaks bread with another." It always comes down to this: our willingness to walk together through the storm and share what we have, so we can create a path to all that matters.

As a hive of bees is incessant in its need to make honey, so are we in our need to make a sweetness of all that we go through. And so being human is loving the particular until it dissolves into the Universal. In time, love shapes us into an instrument that someone suddenly lost might play.

In truth, the agents of kindness are everywhere. I sat in

a café where I live. And there you were. I don't even know your name, but I saw you across the street. You were reaching above you to help a child down from a ledge. It was a complete and absolute kindness. The child was afraid, and you simply smiled and reached. Aware of it or not, you were reaching as one of the tribe of givers who have cared enough to build what we need throughout the ages. Yours is the hand that dragged a stone to finish an aqueduct, the hand that closed a wound on a battlefield, the hand that pulled someone from a temple that was on fire, the hand that held the wailing head of someone in grief. As you lowered the child back to the sidewalk, she scampered away without a word. I watched you watch her vanish back into the stream of the living. Your unexpected moment of kindness gives me hope that we can do what we were put here to do.

It's no surprise that people who love what they do always seem familiar, because when we love, we rise from the same Living Center. And telling stories of those doing what they love enlivens a form of narrative medicine that strengthens the immune system of humanity. The act of loving what we do enables others to love what they do, the way sunlight enables plants to grow.

And that's the job of being kind: to help things grow. Watering seeds can change the world, but the chance to do the watering can change your life. For the heart of gratitude is giving and receiving. This is the exhale and inhale of relationship that keeps us well.

There are many ways to inhabit this ordinary miracle. Instead of waving, the poor farmers in India outside of Puducherry greet strangers by touching their heart. Such a simple way to acknowledge what connects us, such a simple way to water the care between us.

So I encourage you to create your own practice of watering seeds and touching your heart. I encourage you to water the flower you dream of that you wake with in your hand. I encourage you to be there for others so you can discover together what giving and receiving means. I encourage you to tell stories about giving and receiving, especially to young people, so they can inhabit the strength of their kindness, as they take their turn repairing the world.

If blessed on our way from birth to death, we discover our kinship as human beings. And under all our complex thinking and webs of principle and belief, the only moral code that lasts is helping each other up. Under all our dreams and destinations, we simply rush to each other when we fall, the way white blood cells rush to the site of an injury. This is elemental. The health of the world and our souls depends on this simple reflex to stop what we're doing and help.

Once living in the open, there is no career
but being kind.

Questions to Walk With

- For your last journal question, describe one seed you've been watering in the world and how it's growing.

- For your last invitation to be in conversation, meet with a friend or loved one and describe a time when you stopped what you were doing to help another.

52

THE TEMPLE IS THE WORLD

Thousands of candles can be lighted from a single candle, and the life of the candle will not be shortened.

—BUDDHA

SO MUCH TO take in, only to let out. So much to learn, only to accept how little we know. So much to resist, only in the end to surrender. We're refined as we go, made translucent enough to reveal the hidden qualities of being alive. All to regain the simplicity of a dog or a plant. All to find that the space under trouble is our home.

There's one more story, at least for now. A young man determined to find the meaning of life begins his walk in the world. At first, he thinks everything he sees holds the secret. He crosses a river and feels certain that life is like the river, washing us, against our will, into a greater sea. Then he climbs the mountain on the other side of the river and feels certain that life is like the mountain, bare and unmoving the higher we climb. Then he enters a city and feels certain that life is like the crowds of people, everyone so close though we know very little about each other. In time, he starts to forget what he was after.

It's then he meets his teacher, quite unexpectedly. She knows, before he speaks, of all he's seen and wondered. She greets him with this question, "And so do you want to know how all this works, or would you rather apprentice in your true inheritance?"

He doesn't understand all that she says, but her presence makes him stay for several years. They talk in the mornings, but mostly he mimics what she does. After she chops wood, he sharpens the blade. After she empties the water, he goes to fill it. After she talks of the inheritance of being, he asks question after question. And more than finding answers, he grows to love her. This seems to be the answer for everything. Shortly after he grasps this, she dies, as if she were waiting for him to learn how to love, before she left.

In his grief, he tends her chores for months without her. And then in a dream, she whispers, "You must go now and widen your circle." And so he leaves and continues his walk in the world. Except everything is more colorful and he senses the presence of his teacher everywhere. And so he meets everyone with love.

He wanders through cities listening to strangers. He wanders through farm country listening to cows. He wanders into the forest, where he listens to the birds and trees. For all he sought as a young man, he's now finding the same moment, no matter how far he travels. And when the same moment opens, he walks through that moment into the Center of Things. All this makes him terribly sensitive to the plight of others.

In time, a young man like himself finds him and calls him his teacher. He laughs, never thinking of himself this way. But remembering the goodness of his teacher, he gently deflects his student's admiration, saying, "We're only helping each other stay awake."

And so it goes. I wish this journey for you. I hope that everything in the world will speak to you—the river, the mountain, the city, the forest. And I wish you many teachers who will bring you to yourself.

When we lift the pail together, something happens akin to stars sparking in the night. I have run out of ways to describe the journey. Only know this—that in place of wings, God gave us love.

GRATITUDES

EACH BOOK IS a surprise in how it calls and unfolds, never quite what I imagine. And I'm grateful for what each book opens, and how each transforms me. And especially grateful for those who understand when the journey makes me inward or giddy or somewhat lost. I'm grateful to my agent Jennifer Rudolph Walsh for her unfailing encouragement inwardly and support in the world, as well as for Eve Attermann, who is wise beyond her years, and James Munro, Fiona Baird, and the rest of the WME team for their care and excellence. And to my publisher and editor, Joel Fotinos for his vision and care and true collaboration. And to Brooke Warner for her steadfast friendship and keen understanding. And to my publicist Eileen Duhne for her kindness and good will.

My path is filled with friends. So deep gratitude to my dear friends for who they are and what they share. Especially George, Don, Paul, Skip, TC, David, Kurt, Pam, Karen, Paula, Ellen, Parker, Dave, Jill, Jacquelyn, Linda, Michelle, Rich, Carolyn,

Henk, Sandra, Elesa, Penny, and Joel and Sally. And to Oprah Winfrey, for how she repairs the temple that is the world.

And to Paul Bowler, who's been an inner explorer his whole life. And to my dear old friend, Robert Mason, whose eyes were a gateway the minute we met. And to my wife, Susan, who rides the sail of her huge heart, helping everyone she meets.

Notes

Epigraphs and poems with the initials MN are by the author.

p. ix, epigraphs **"Don't you want"**: From Anthony Doerr. *All the Light We Cannot See* (New York: Scribner, 2014), 270.

p. ix, **"Who will speak these days"**: From Muriel Rukeyser, "The Speed of Darkness," in *The Speed of Darkness* (New York: Random House, 1968).

WHERE ALL SOULS MEET

p. xvi **by way of a journal.** For an in-depth guide into the art of journaling, including 100 journal questions to work with, please see my book *Things That Join the Sea and the Sky: Field Notes on Living.* Sounds True, 2017.

OUR WALK IN THE WORLD

p. 1, epigraph **"The more you cut the branches"**: From Abdul-Baha, quoted in *The Sun*, issue 478 (October 2015): 48.

1. LIVING WITH MEANING, TRUTH, AND KINDNESS

p. 5, epigraph **"We are people hungry for life"**: From Robert Seder, *To The Marrow* (CavanKerry Press, 2006). *To the Marrow* is Robert Seder's intimate and searing journal of his five-year journey through a bone-marrow transplant. I was privileged to write the foreword to this remarkable account.

5. THE PULL of EXISTENCE

p. 24 **"Our present education"**: From *J. Krishnamurti, The Book of Life* (San Francisco: HarperOne, 1995).

6. BEING WHOLEHEARTED

p. 26, epigraph **"Why not call the moment of certainty"**: From "Utterance-That-Rises-Briefly-From-The-Source," in my book of poems *The Way Under the Way: The Place of True Meeting* (Boulder, CO: Sounds True, 2016), 94.

p. 27 **the shadow:** Entering the work of Carl Jung is like entering an entire universe. To introduce yourself, please see *Modern Man in Search of a Soul; The Undiscovered Self; Memories, Dreams, Reflections* (his autobiography); or *The Portable Jung*, edited by Joseph Campbell. For contemporary work on the shadow, please see Robert A. Johnson's *Owning Your Own Shadow: Understanding the Dark Side of the Psyche*.

p. 28 **"As long as we refuse"**: From Jean Vanier. See such Vanier classics as *Community and Growth, Becoming Human,* and *The Heart of L'Arche: A Spirituality for Every Day*.

p. 29 **"I am the twelve-year-old girl"**: From Thich Nhat Hanh, "Please Call Me by My True Names," in *Call Me by My True Names: The Collected Poems of Thich Nhat Hanh* (Berkeley, CA: Parallax Press, 1999), 72.

7. PUSHING ON

p. 32, epigraph **"You don't need to be without fear"**: Tami Simon is a dear friend. She is the founder of Sounds True. This is from her wise audio program *Being True*.

8. AS MANY TIMES AS NECESSARY

p. 36 "We shall not cease from exploration": From T. S. Eliot, "Little Gidding" in *Four Quartets* (New York: Mariner Books, 1968).

11. ORIGINAL STEPS

p. 51, epigraph "A bull contents himself": From Seneca the Younger, quoted in *Lapham's Quarterly* 5, no. 2 (Animals Issue, Spring 2013): 20.

p. 51 "The newly discovered lines to the epic": Details about the newly discovered Gilgamesh tablet are from a superb article, which includes the entire text of the tablet both transliterated and translated into English, published by Farouk Al-Rawi and Andrew George of the University of London's School of Oriental and African Studies, http://www .thehistoryblog.com/wp-content/uploads/2015/09/jcunestud.66.0069_w -footer.pdf, and from *The History Blog,* http://www.thehistoryblog.com /archives/38631.

12. DISTRIBUTING THE WEIGHT

p. 55, epigraph "Everybody's hurt": From a talk James Baldwin gave in the fall of 1962 at New York City's Community Church, which was broadcast on WBAI on November 29 under the title "The Artist's Struggle for Integrity."

p. 56 "In the Milky Ocean": From my book *The Way Under The Way: The Place of True Meeting* (Boulder, CO: Sounds True, 2016), 161.

OUR TRUE INHERITANCE

p. 63 "The waking have one common world…" Heraclitus, in *Early Greek Philosophy* by John Burnet, 3rd edition, 1920 (fragment 89).

14. THE FIRE OF ALIVENESS

p. 67, epigraph "There was that law of life": From Norman Mailer, quoted in *The Sun*, issue 387 (March 2008): 48.

p. 67, epigraph "In the Judaic tradition": From Gail Godwin, *Heart* (New York: William Morrow, 2001), 29.

p. 68 **the naked freedom of a star . . . a fish gulping for food at the surface:** The images toward the end of this paragraph and in the beginning of the next were first explored in my poem "The Promise of the Inner World" in my book *Reduced to Joy* (Berkeley, CA: Viva Editions, 2013), 135.

p. 69 **"As my prayer became more attentive and inward":** From Søren Kierkegaard, quoted in *The Sun*, issue 376 (April 2007): 48.

p. 71 **"That's how we measure out our real respect":** From Ted Hughes, *Letters of Ted Hughes,* ed. Christopher Reid (New York: Farrar, Straus & Giroux, 2007).

15. THE SLOWING OF THE LAND

p. 74, epigraph **"There is a day":** From Wendell Berry, *The Selected Poems of Wendell Berry* (Berkeley CA: Counterpoint Press, 1999.

16. STAYING POSSIBLE

p. 77, epigraph **"I test the limits of myself":** Many of the quotes and details in this chapter about Marina Abramović come from the excellent article by Sean O'Hagan, "Interview: Marina Abramović," in *The Guardian/The Observer,* Saturday, October 2, 2010; the Museum of Modern Art website, www.moma.org/interactives/exhibitions/2010/marinaabramovic/; and from *Marina Abramović,* ed. A Daneri (Milan, Italy: Charta, 2002), 29–30, 35.

p. 78 *The Artist Is Present:* I highly recommend the HBO documentary *The Artist Is Present* (directed by Jeff Dupre, 2012) which portrays the living exhibit and retrospective while tracing the life and art of Marina Abramović, www.hbo.com/documentaries/marina-abramovic-the-artist-is -present/index.htm.

17. LESSENING FEAR

p. 83, epigraph **"A person who is beginning":** From Ken Wilbur, quoted in *The Sun,* issue 487 (July 2016): 48.

18. WHAT TO BRING FORWARD

p. 91, epigraph **"If you can understand":** From Edward B. Burger, *Coincidences, Chaos, and All That Math Jazz: Making Light of Weighty Ideas* (New

York: W. W. Norton, 2005). Burger is a professor of mathematics and the department chair at Williams College.

19. OUR ORIGINAL TALENT

p. 98, epigraph "**Dive into the ocean**": From Attar, quoted in *Sufi, A Journal of Sufism*. London: Khaniqahi Nimatullahi Publications, issue 91 (Summer 2016): 10.

p. 100 **Bernice Johnson Reagon . . . movement:** Keynote speaker, honoring Martin Luther King, Jr., Day, Stetson Chapel, Kalamazoo College, January 16, 2012.

21. THE ART OF BEING SENSITIVE

p. 107 **The Art of Being Sensitive:** An abridged version of this chapter appeared in *Spirituality & Health Magazine*, March/April 2017.

p. 107, epigraph "**The artist's struggle**": From a talk James Baldwin gave in the fall of 1962 at New York City's Community Church, which was broadcast on WBAI on November 29 under the title "The Artist's Struggle for Integrity."

p. 108 **Chopin nocturne:** The Polish composer Frédéric Chopin (1810–1849) composed twenty-one nocturnes, short pieces for solo piano written between 1827 and 1846. These intense compositions are considered among the finest short solo works ever created for piano. Chopin expanded on the nocturne, building on the form created by the Irish composer John Field.

22. CHASING PARADISE

p. 111, epigraph "**The only protection I can offer**": From Emad Burnat, a Palestinian photographer, the writer and director of *Five Broken Cameras* (2007), a documentary that chronicles the struggle of his hometown of Bil'in as a border town brutally divided and quarantined by the Israeli wall.

p. 111 **chasing Paradise:** I first explored this notion in the chapter "Meeting Difficulty" in my book *The Endless Practice* (New York: Atria Books, 2014), 68.

p. 112 **"[People] will get angry"**: From Jacquelyn Vincenta, *The Lake and the Lost Girl* (Naperville, IL: Sourcebooks, 2017), 91.

p. 112 **In the 1960s . . . "'improvident'"**: From George Foster, *Premises Underlying the Efforts of the Wildflowers Institute* (unpublished paper), p. 3; originally cited in Melford Spiro, "Buddhism and Economic Behavior in Burma," *American Anthropologist* 68: 63–73.

23. AS WE KEEP SEARCHING

p. 118 **finding our courage:** For an in-depth exploration of inner courage, please see my book *Finding Inner Courage* (San Francisco: Conari Press, 2011).

WIDENING OUR CIRCLE

p. 133, epigraph **"I have walked through many lives"**: From Stanley Kunitz, "The Layers," in *The Poems of Stanley Kunitz 1928–1978* (Boston: Little, Brown, 1979), 35.

p. 135, headnote: **"A human being is a part of the whole…"** *The Quantum and the Lotus: A Journey to the Frontiers Where Science and Buddhism Meet* by Matthieu Ricard and Trinh Xuan Thuan. NY: Broadway Books, 2004. This excerpt is from a letter of consolation that Einstein wrote in February 1950 to Robert S. Marcus, whose young son had just died of polio.

28. THE COVENANT OF PRACTICE

p. 141 **"The role of spiritual practice"**: From "Who Hears This Sound?" an interview with Adyashanti by Luc Saunders and Sy Safransky, in *The Sun,* issue 384 (December 2007). I used this quote as well in the chapter "Outwaiting the Clouds" in my book *Seven Thousand Ways to Listen* (New York: Atria Books, 2013).

p. 144 **"the other, greater beauty"**: From Rainer Maria Rilke, *Auguste Rodin* (New York: Dover Publications, 2006) 7. This is one of the most remarkable explorations of the nature of creativity written by a great poet

as he watched a great sculptor work up close. Rilke worked as Rodin's sec-
retary in the early 1900s. This book is comprised of two profound personal
essays published by Rilke in 1903 and 1907.

29. UNWAVERING

p. 146 **a dog named Hachikō:** Details about Hachikō's life are taken from
Barbara Bouyet, *Akita: Treasure of Japan,* vol. 2 (Hong Kong: Magnum
Publishing, 2002), 5–7.

p. 148 **Zuzu's petals:** Detail drawn from the Urban Dictionary, http://
www.urbandictionary.com/define.php?term=Zuzu%27s%20Petals.

30. HONORING THE ANONYMOUS

p. 149, epigraph **"We draw the circle of our family too small":** From
Mother Teresa, quoted in David Addiss, "Spiritual Themes and Challenges
in Global Health"; originally cited in Steve Reifenberg, "Afterword," in *In
the Company of the Poor: Conversations with Dr. Paul Farmer and Fr. Gus-
tavo Gutierrez*, ed. Michael Griffin and Jennie Weiss Block (Maryknoll,
NY: Orbis Books, 2013), 189–197.

p. 150 **"Name Withheld":** From Sy Safransky, *The Sun,* issue 457 (January
2014), 27–28.

31. LOOKING AT THINGS FRESHLY

p. 156 **"[He] used to talk about the value":** From Carol Lee Flinders, "Our
Spiritual Genealogy: A Conversation with Carol Lee Flinders," in *Sufi, A
Journal of Sufism*, issue 91 (Summer 2016), 22.

32. A CHILD OF THE SIXTIES

p. 159 **A Child of the Sixties:** For an intimate documentary about the sixties, please see *Sean* (2006) by writer-director Ralph Arlyck, which begins
with a conversation with four-year-old Sean Farrell, the son of free-spirited
parents living in 1969 in San Francisco's Haight-Ashbury neighborhood.
Arlyck revisits Sean and his parents thirty years later, reflecting on his own
life journey along the way.

33. PROSPERITY BLINDNESS

p. 162, epigraph "The human race has had": From Alan Gregg, quoted in the journal *The Sun,* issue 370 (October 2006), 48.

p. 165 **Wildflowers Institute:** Established in 1997 by Hanmin Liu, Wildflowers Institute (www.wildflowers.org) is a social-innovation and application lab focused on understanding how communities work. The aim of the institute is to design methods and tools to catalyze the innate power in communities. The institute's work is based on the belief that the greatest promise for self-sustaining community change comes from strengthening the existing resources within the community.

p. 167 **"To be is more essential than to have":** From Abraham Joshua Heschel, *The Earth Is the Lord's: The Inner World of the Jew in Eastern Europe* (Woodstock, VT: Jewish Lights Publishing, 2001), 14.

34. THE WANTING PLACE

p. 168, epigraph **"When I see":** From Eddie Cantor, quoted in *The Sun,* issue 47, (June 2015), 48.

p. 168 **"In Spanish, *querencia*":** From Georgia Heard, *Writing Toward Home* (Portsmouth, NH: Heinemann, 1995).

35. THE CONSTANT UNFOLDING

p. 171, epigraph **"Only whose vision":** From E. E. Cummings, "Only whose vision can create the whole," in *100 Selected Poems* (New York: Grove Press, 1959), 99.

36. FOUR SMALL LESSONS

p. 177 **Between 1934 and 1939 . . . because of his photograph:** Details from the compelling exhibit *Roman Vishniac Rediscovered,* at International Center of Photography, New York City, March 10, 2013.

37. OUR ORBIT OF CONCERN

p. 180: **"There's a lot of talk in this country..."** Barack Obama, an excerpt from his commencement address at Northwestern University in June, 2006, https://www.northwestern.edu/newscenter/stories/2006/06/barack.html.

38. GLIDE, PULL, WALK, AND CARRY

p. 185 "The place specifically where all my family is from": From Alex Wilson, "Showing Love in Our Actions" in *Sufi,* issue 91 (Summer 2016), 32.

HELPING EACH OTHER STAY AWAKE

p. 193, epigraph **"Now, I have no choice":** From Yannis Ritsos, "Necessary Explanation," in *Yannis Ritsos: Selected Poems 1938–1988,* trans. Kimon Friar and Kostas Myrsiades (Brockport, NY: BOA Editions, 1989), 25. Yannis Ritsos (1909–1990) is one of the legendary modern Greek poets. Both profound and prolific, Ritsos authored more than 117 books of poetry, translations, fiction, essays, and drama. This seminal collection includes over twenty-five illustrations of the poet's paintings on rocks.

p. 193, epigraph **"Remaking the treasure for another":** Margo McLoughlin is a dear friend and amazing storyteller, http://www.margostoryteller.net.

p. 195 **"We begin life":** From Sally Z. Hare, *The Journey from Knowing about Community to Knowing Community,* (March 2005), 4.

40. HOW DAY FOLLOWS NIGHT

p. 197, epigraph **"The hero is [the one]":** From Ralph Waldo Emerson, in Rainer Maria Rilke, *Auguste Rodin* (New York: Dover Publications, 2006), viii.

41. EACH TIME I BEGIN

p. 200 *The Age of Bronze:* The sculpture *The Age of Bronze* by Auguste Rodin seems to breathe in the center of a sunlit hall in New York's Metropolitan Museum of Art. Rodin completed the sculpture in Paris in 1876.

42. THE FINITUDES

p. 205 **I stumble on Martin Heidegger's notion of dwelling . . . everything:** Martin Heidegger (1889–1976) was an influential German philosopher known for his explorations of the question of being. His best-known book, *Being and Time,* is considered an important philosophical work of the twentieth century.

p. 205 **only to discover he supported Hitler . . . rector:** Heidegger joined the Nazi Party on May 1, 1933, nearly three weeks after being appointed rector of the University of Freiburg. Heidegger resigned about one year later, in April 1934, but remained a member of the Nazi Party until the end of World War II. His first act as rector was to eliminate all democratic structures, including those that had elected him rector. There were book burnings on his campus, some of which he successfully stopped, as well as some student violence.

p. 205 **It's taken over sixty years . . . to the beginning:** Parts of the opening two paragraphs originally appeared in an earlier version as a poem called "The Finitudes" in my book *The Way Under the Way: The Place of True Meeting* (Boulder, CO: Sounds True, 2016), 58.

p. 206 **Hannah Arendt . . . after the war:** Arendt (1906–1975) was an influential German Jewish political theorist and a student of Martin Heidegger. Her best-known works are *The Human Condition* (1958) and *Eichmann in Jerusalem: A Report on the Banality of Evil* (1963). Immigrating to the United States from Germany in 1941, she became the first female professor at Princeton University in 1969.

p. 208 **"I would argue":** Please see Parker Palmer, "The Politics of the Broken-Hearted: On Holding the Tensions of Democracy," in *Deepening the American Dream,* ed. Mark Nepo (San Francisco, CA: Jossey-Bass, 2005), p. 231–257. This quote is from a conversation with Parker early in the writing of this book.

44. THE GREATER PRAYER OF BEING

p. 213, epigraph **"In Quakerism":** From an interview with Parker Palmer by Alicia Von Stamwitz, "If Only We Would Listen," in *The Sun,* issue 443 (November 2012), 12.

45. AN INNER RIGHT-OF-WAY

p. 218 **"intimacy as the proving ground for the conscious heart":** Carolyn Rivers and Henk Brandt have created *The Sophia Institute* (www .thesophiainstitute.org) in Charleston, South Carolina, where leading teachers and artists from around the country convene creative individuals to explore personal and relational transformation as it impacts the awakening of the conscious heart. I have been blessed to teach and present there for more than a decade. It is an outstanding community of seekers worth joining.

p. 219 **George Nakashima:** Details about the life of George Nakashima are from an exhibit at The Metropolitan Museum of Art in New York City of his legendary *Table, Conoid Lounge Chairs, and Greenrock Benches* (1986–1987), made of American walnut.

p. 220 **Abenake elder Joseph Bruchac:** This notion is from a dialogue I had with Joe Bruchac in March 2007. For an invaluable introduction to the Native American worldview, please see his *Our Stories Remember: Indian History, Culture, and Values through Storytelling* (New York: Golden, CO: Fulcrum Publishing, 2003).

p. 220 **Joseph Haydn:** Haydn (1732–1809) was a prolific Austrian composer of the classical period. He was instrumental in the development of chamber music and is considered one of the fathers of the symphony. Young Beethoven was a student of his. In 1806, at the age of seventy-four, unable to go to the piano anymore, Haydn said, "Usually musical ideas are pursuing me, to the point of torture, I cannot escape them. . . . My imagination plays on me as if I were a clavier. . . . I am really just a living clavier." This quote is from Albert Christoph Dies, "Biographical Accounts of Joseph Haydn" (from 1810), in *Haydn: Two Contemporary Portraits*, trans. and ed. Vernon Gotwals (Milwaukee: University of Wisconsin Press, 1963). A clavier is an early form of keyboard, a precursor to the piano, more like a harpsichord.

p. 221 **It was a mild summer night . . . that day:** Details about the "Farewell" Symphony (Symphony No. 45 in F-sharp minor) are from https://en.wikipedia.org/wiki/Symphony_No._45_(Haydn).

48. WHAT IF?

p. 232, epigraph **"Who looks outside":** From Carl Jung, *Memories, Dreams, Reflections,* ed. Aniela Jaffe (New York: Random House, 1961).

p. 233 **"What if you slept":** From the poem "What Then?" in *The Selected Poetry of Samuel Taylor Coleridge,* ed. H. J. Jackson (London: Oxford University Press, 2009).

49. TRY, ACCEPT, BEGIN AGAIN

p. 236, epigraph **"When an imperative arises"**: Tami Simon is a dear friend. She is the founder of Sounds True. This is from her wise audio program *Being True*.

50. THE FRAGRANT CLIFF

p. 240 **Afraid of dying, . . . "After you die, what will you need?"**: This is the beginning of the eighteenth case in the legendary *Blue Cliff Record*, a compilation of one hundred koans with commentaries, a Zen Talmud of sorts, begun by Dōgen (1200–1253) and added to by many voices through the years. *The Blue Cliff Record,* trans. Thomas Cleary and J. C. Cleary (Boston: Shambhala, 2005), 115.

51. THE AGENTS OF KINDNESS

p. 243, epigraph **"What keeps buildings and forests"**: From Elizabeth Lesser, *Marrow* (New York: HarperCollins, 2016), 306.

52. THE TEMPLE IS THE WORLD

p. 248: **"Thousands of candles..."** attributed to Buddha, a paraphrase of Section 10 of the "Sutra of 42 Sections" in a Japanese text, *The Teaching of Buddha.*

PERMISSIONS

About the Author

With over A million copies sold, **MARK NEPO** has moved and inspired readers and seekers all over the world with his #1 *New York Times* best seller *The Book of Awakening*. Beloved as a poet, teacher, and storyteller, Mark has been called "one of the finest spiritual guides of our time," "a consummate storyteller," and "an eloquent spiritual teacher." His work is widely accessible and used by many, and his books have been translated into more than twenty languages. A best-selling author, he has published twenty-two books and recorded fifteen audio projects. In 2015, he was given a Life Achievement Award by AgeNation. In 2016, he was named by *Watkins: Mind Body Spirit* as one of the 100 Most Spiritually Influential Living People, and was also chosen as one of Oprah Winfrey Network's (OWN's) SuperSoul 100, a group of inspired leaders using their gifts and voices to elevate humanity. And in 2017 Mark became a regular columnist for *Spirituality & Health* magazine.

Recent work includes *Drinking from the River of Light* (Sounds True, 2019); *More Together Than Alone* (Atria, 2018), cited by *Spirituality & Practice* as one of the Best Spiritual Books of 2018; *Things That Join the Sea and the Sky* (Sounds True, 2017), a Nautilus Book Award winner; *The Way Under the Way: The Place of True Meeting* (Sounds True, 2016), a Nautilus Book Award winner; *The One Life We're Given* (Atria), cited by *Spirituality & Practice* as one of the Best Spiritual Books of 2016; *Inside the Miracle* (Sounds True), selected by *Spirituality & Health Magazine* as one of the top ten best books of 2015; *The Endless Practice* (Atria), cited by *Spirituality & Practice* as one of the Best Spiritual Books of 2014; and *Seven Thousand Ways to Listen* (Atria), which won the 2012 Books for a Better Life Award.

Mark was part of Oprah Winfrey's The Life You Want Tour in 2014 and has appeared several times with Oprah on her *Super Soul Sunday* program on OWN TV. He has also been interviewed by Robin Roberts on *Good Morning America*. *The Exquisite Risk* was listed by *Spirituality & Practice* as one of the Best Spiritual Books of 2005, calling it "one of the best books we've ever read on what it takes to live an authentic life." Mark devotes his writing and teaching to the journey of inner transformation and the life of relationship. He continues to offer readings, lectures, and retreats. Please visit Mark at: www.marknepo.com, http://threeintentions.com, and http://wmespeakers.com/speaker/mark-nepo.

The purpose of any dream is to exercise the heart until it awakens.